The Darcy Myth

THE

Darcy Myth

JANE AUSTEN, LITERARY HEARTTHROBS, AND THE MONSTERS THEY TAUGHT US TO LOVE

RACHEL FEDER

QUIRK BOOKS

PHILADELPHIA

Library of Congress Cataloging-in-Publication Data
Names: Feder, Rachel, author.
Title: The Darcy myth : Jane Austen, literary heartthrobs, and the monsters they taught us to love / Rachel Feder.
Description: Philadelphia : Quirk Books, [2023] | Includes bibliographical references and index. | Summary: "An examination of how the romantic narrative from Pride and Prejudice was born out of Gothic horror, how it influenced pop culture since its publishing, and how it has reinforced harmful cultural concepts of real-life romance"—Provided by publisher.
Identifiers: LCCN 2023005040 (print) | LCCN 2023005041 (ebook) | ISBN 9781683693574 (paperback) | ISBN 9781683693581 (ebook)
Subjects: LCSH: Austen, Jane, 1775-1817. Pride and prejudice. | Austen, Jane, 1775-1817—Characters. | Darcy, Fitzwilliam (Fictitious character) | Libertines in literature. | LCGFT: Literary criticism.
Classification: LCC PR4034.P73 F43 2023 (print) | LCC PR4034.P73 (ebook) | DDC 823/.7—dc23/eng/20230315
LC record available at https://lccn.loc.gov/2023005040
LC ebook record available at https://lccn.loc.gov/2023005041

ISBN: 978-1-68369-357-4

Printed in China

Typeset in Baskerville, Woolen, Rivina, and Brother 1816

Designed by Elissa Flanigan
Cover illustration credit: Shutterstock/Magic Panda
Production management by John J. McGurk

Quirk Books
215 Church Street
Philadelphia, PA 19106
quirkbooks.com

10 9 8 7 6 5 4 3 2 1

For my parents, Rob and Andee Feder,
who taught me not to take any shit

Contents

Prologue:
OF KITTENS
AND
MUTTON
CHOPS

I just stepped out of a juniper bush.

Let me paint you a picture, then spin you a yarn. At the moment, I'm sitting under the big, old ash tree in my yard, branches quite literally tangled in my hair, little bits of spiky evergreen and fluffy seeds all over my fleece. (I say *my* fleece, but it is actually my brother's fleece jacket from middle school, which has, in this hectic October, become my capsule wardrobe.)

About an hour ago, I received a text from my thirteen-year-old neighbor Julie. There was a cat, she said. At least, she thought it was a cat. It sounded hurt. She couldn't see it. It was in a juniper bush outside her house.

Now, let me be clear. I do not have free time right now. I'm not complaining; I'm just explaining. And it's not like I buy into capitalist hustle culture or anything, I'm just having a busy fall. I have 501 unread emails. I have 361 unread texts. I am not a particularly important person, except to my children, who didn't send me any of the emails, and I guess to my students, who did. I am not bragging, and am in fact embarrassed to tell you these things about myself. (Our iPhones, ourselves.) I just need to make very clear, for the thrust of my argument, that I needed to use this time while my husband took the kids to get their flu shots to work on writing this very book.

But did I suggest Julie call the animal shelter, turn my phone on do not disturb, and get to work? No, I absolutely did not.

She sent me a video. It was a video of a juniper bush just sitting there, being a juniper bush, except for one distinctive feature: a plaintive, mysterious cry.

Now, am I the right person to go check out a cat mystery? Also no. I have no qualifications. I love cats but have never had a cat. I don't really understand them. They seem to hate me? Nothing is off-limits to them? And yet they never want to snuggle? The point is, I have absolutely no idea how to even ascertain the lost-ness of a cat, let alone catch one and tend to its possible wounds.

And yet, after a few texts back and forth, my intentions started to solidify, like butter and sugar beginning to caramelize.

You see, I was once that teenage girl fully phenomenologically oriented toward the project of rescuing little creatures in distress. My kindergarten bestie and I frequently dedicated entire days to creating a bespoke storybook (words by me, pictures by her) in which we found and acquired companion animals of all kinds. In my time on this earth, I have found a lot of lost dogs—or, rather, they seemed to have found me. Temporary pets of my girlhood included a field mouse I caught *inside the house*, a horned lizard, and multiple salamanders. (I may have accidentally transported that mouse home from the barn.) You want turtle tales? I've got plenty. Did I somehow end up with a geriatric rabbit living in my dorm room in my freshman year of college? That one is a long story, and her name was Lola. Did I let my kids keep a hand-me-down hermit crab that was a decade old and the size of a slider? Yes, and I made him little organic salads.

All of this is to say that the fantasy of rescuing a helpless animal and turning him or her into my magical little friend is deeply ingrained in my bones. And when that storyline was activated—even though I had work to do, and wasn't the best person for the job—I came running.

This is a book about Mr. Darcy. You'll understand the connection in a minute.

I'm an English professor at a small university in Colorado and an expert on British literature. While I've never been a dedicated Jane Austen fan, or Janeitc, per se (I'm more a *Frankenstein* and *Dracula* kind of girl), I teach a course on Jane Austen almost every year. And every year, I ruin *Pride and Prejudice*.

When I say "ruin," I don't mean the way you might, say, ruin a silk blouse by chasing a cat into a juniper bush. I mean the way you might ruin the song "Total Eclipse of the Heart" by telling someone that Bonnie Tyler originally meant it to be about vampires (this is true). I've now upended whatever uncomplicated associations you had with this song, and you'll never be able to hear it without thinking of vampires again, but I've made it much more *interesting*. Anyway, English professors have lots of tools at our disposal for ruining your favorite books, and the way I prefer to ruin *Pride and Prejudice* is by pointing out how literature trains women to spend their time changing assholes into sensitive men instead of overthrowing the patriarchy.

Now, don't get me wrong: I love *Pride and Prejudice*! I love it on the page and I love it on film, and I maybe love it even more because I love ruining it so much. And as far as I can tell, my students like me even though I ruin it. They tell me I'm "relatable" and "super sweet and nerdy" (this was in an anonymous online review, and honestly, how very dare you). They also once said I was "the best birth control." (That was when I was hugely, embarrassingly pregnant. Like, I texted a picture of myself to one of my best friends and instead of responding with "you're glowing" or even "so excited," she wrote back, "you look like a UFO.") The birth control comment is not really related to my habit of ruining *Pride and Prejudice*, but I think it gives you a sense of what it's like to study Jane Austen with me. That is, taking a class with me is all fun and games until you're hugging your roommate in the English department lounge because you realized that you've been spending your time and energy and attention on taciturn or emotionally unavailable people, believing they are going to turn out to be slow-burn romantic heroes like Mr. Darcy—when really, they are often just assholes.

So many of us are vulnerable to this fallacy. We think that if we're sufficiently docile, patient, charming, useful, and/or conciliatory, we can melt the heart of any standoffish love interest, turning them into a devoted and attentive suitor. Why do we believe, against all evidence, that someone who's constantly low-key negging us and only texts back after midnight is suddenly going to turn into Mr. Darcy?

We think this because of fucking Darcy, that's why! Literature is full of lies.

I'm not trying to lay all of this on Jane Austen's shoulders. The myth of the haughty crush turned romantic hero has been so influential that it's still being repeated in current culture. Take *Bridgerton*, for instance, the recent Netflix series based on the Regency romance novels of Julia Quinn. I stayed up all night binging the first season of *Bridgerton*, don't get me wrong, but it is super complicit in this bullshit. The heroine, Daphne Bridgerton, is being actively courted by an actual charming prince, but passes him over for a duke with serious daddy issues who can't quite bring himself to express emotions or vulnerability for, oh, most of the show. I mean, the prince is *right there.* It's not like pursuing a relationship with the prince would involve some radical reimagining of the social structure. It wouldn't even involve Daphne standing up to her hypocritical, domineering older brother! (I love Anthony Bridgerton, by the way. I feel for him and I want to hug him and make him soup—because society has broken me.) Prince Friedrich is a *literal prince.* A prince who is attentive and confident, yet prioritizes his partner's needs. Sure, he insists he simply must have the first dance, but he also makes sure to clarify before proposing that he'd be happy to settle near Daphne's family! Friedrich is a prince in every sense. But . . . his mutton chops are kind of weird. He doesn't make her feel *that thing*, you know, that weird, confused, longing, lustful ache that emotionally unavailable people learn how to conjure because they want to feel wanted but also need to know they're safe from having to be in an actual relationship. You know, the thing she feels for the emotionally unavailable duke.

Spoiler alert, but you know what happens next. The moody duke rejects Daphne. Then he hooks up with her. Then he rejects her again. Then there's a duel and she saves him and he ignores her and tortures her and marries her and provides the sum total of her sexual

Meet a Darcy

NAME:	Simon Bassett, the Duke of Hastings
LOVE STORY:	Season 1 of *Bridgerton*
TURN-ONS:	Sexual experience, helping sexually inexperienced women become *more* experienced, witty banter, oil paintings, deep friendship
TURN-OFFS:	The idea of getting somebody pregnant, thus accidentally carrying on his father's legacy

This duke is *so hot*, it almost doesn't matter that he says he would rather die than marry you, or that he later claims he only said that because he couldn't give you children but then gaslights you about where babies come from. He is the kind of hot that makes you question the very definition of art and the nature of the human form.

But this dashing duke has a dark past. His father was cruel, neglectful, and ableist and refused to forge an emotional bond with his son, who had a speech impediment in childhood. At his father's deathbed, to punish his father for his misdeeds, Simon promised that he would never produce an heir, and that the title of Duke—the only thing his father cared about—would die with him. But the duke might be able to overcome his traumatic past, and this dark promise, if the woman he loves is patient, caring, and forgiving enough. Could that be you?

education which involves a lot of deceit followed by a revenge rape.

Daphne, the prince was right there, seriously! If you can't see past his mutton chops, just ask if he'll shave them—you know he would, for you. And then you'd see what those of us with Google already know, which is that a clean-shaven Freddie Stroma is hot, if you like classic beefcake. Plus, it would probably be a nice loving consensual sexual relationship from the start!

But of course, animated as it is by what I'm calling the Darcy myth, *Bridgerton* shows us that Daphne was right all along. First, the viewer learns the duke's tragic backstory—rejection by an abusive father—and thus sympathizes with his low-key cruel tendencies. Then Daphne discovers his secret, in the form of a literal packet of letters that his father never opened but kept for some reason, and shows him the light by expressing her love and understanding while looking gorgeous in the rain. Daphne gets her duke and her love story and her baby by following her heart, putting up with and even participating in abuse, and just kind of waiting it out. Her beauty, her sensitivity, her empathy, and her patience turn the beast back into the prince he was always meant to be.

And as for the prince who was right there all along? Well, his love isn't worth as much, because it doesn't have to be earned.

Here's where the cat comes in. Charging into that juniper bush, imagining myself as the beloved savior and forever companion of an animal I *did not know* and had *no idea how to care for,* I realized that I was essentially being puppeteered by the narratives I imprinted on as a child. The stories we're brought up on are more than just stories. They become our personal mythologies. They burrow deep in our marrow.

The idea that I would someday rescue an adorable creature who would then become my pet came to me from the books I read, the films I watched in childhood. Thinking back, it's hard to pinpoint a specific example. The works of James Herriot, maybe? All those horse girl and kid-and-dog books I devoured? Something about Disney princesses moving among the animals? It's hard to say for sure.

The Darcy myth is a story like this: a simple dynamic with huge emotional payoff that we internalize before we've even realized what's happening. I'll discuss *Pride and Prejudice* in more depth in the following chapters, but in a nutshell, Austen's classic novel and the endless iterations of the slow-burn, enemies-to-lovers romance plot she perfected therein teach us a story. The story goes: There will be someone you just can't stand. You will be warned that they are bad, and your initial impression will corroborate the rumors. This is the beginning of your great love.

You'd think that once we grew up and became self-aware, the Darcy myth would loosen its hold on us. We'd take our romances as they came, and not relate to them within the framework of dominant cultural archetypes. But until we acknowledge the Darcy myth, we can't divest from it. Until we understand how the Darcy myth has influenced our thoughts, feelings, and actions until we've reconsidered these stories, and even shared them with one another to see how we've all been mind-fucked by the same myth—we can never truly be free.

The work of this book is to look the Darcy myth straight in its smoldering eyes so that we can take what we need from it and leave the rest behind. Because sometimes we act based on our belief in a story, even though we think we know better.

I reached out my hand and closed my fingers around the kitten's tail. But much like Mr. Darcy always does, she slipped through my fingers.

PART ONE

How Love Became a
SCARY STORY

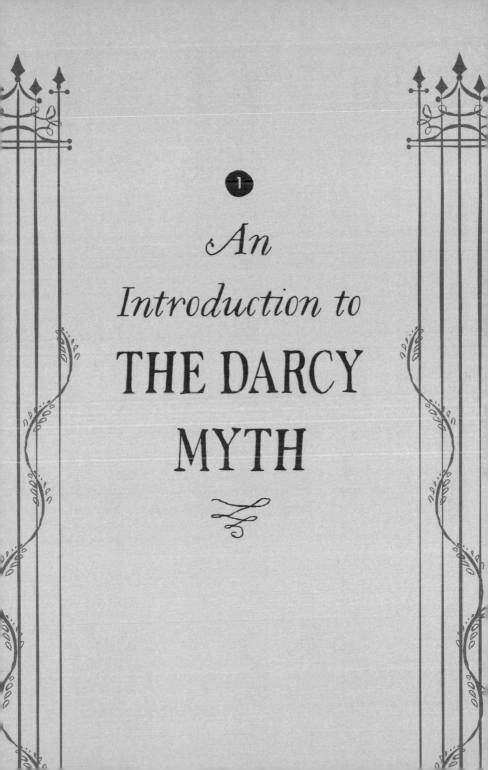

1

An Introduction to THE DARCY MYTH

*M*y students first drew my attention to the connection between *Pride and Prejudice* and the work of Sally Rooney, the best-selling author of *Normal People* and *Conversations with Friends*—essentially romance-focused novels with a literary gloss. One student, Eleanor, suggested that *Normal People* follows a similar arc to *Pride and Prejudice* insofar as the main characters are "kind of terrible to each other in the beginning and then they have to slowly, slowly start warming up towards each other and they're like, oh my god, I'm in love." My colleague Gloria Fisk, who studies contemporary literature, agrees with Eleanor's assessment; in a recent essay, she writes that "the realist novel would be nowhere without the stories of young white women falling in love, and Sally Rooney writes about nothing else." (We'll discuss later what context we miss when we treat Jane Austen as an originator and prime example of "the realist novel," but this is a common genre definition for Austen, and one of the axes along which Fisk is connecting Austen to Rooney.)

In her essay on Rooney, and in a later conversation about the subject, Fisk brings up Janice Radway's 1984 book *Reading the Romance: Women, Patriarchy, and Popular Culture*. To write the book, which is now somewhat dated but was groundbreaking in its time, Radway interviewed avid readers of romance novels in order to understand what they got from their reading lives. One trope Radway analyzed dovetails with the plot of *Pride and Prejudice*: the heroine initially dislikes a man because he is arrogant and mean, then gains some new piece of information about him that makes his behavior make sense. Summarizing Radway, Fisk explained that, through this plot arc, romance novels rationalize women's ill treatment under patriarchy, suggesting that a man who treats you poorly is just hurt, and waiting to be understood and loved.

Now, let me be clear. I love genre fiction. (Not unrelatedly, as you will learn, I also know too much about reality TV.) I don't think there's any shame in saying that Sally Rooney books are highbrow

Meet a Darcy

NAME: Connell Waldron

LOVE STORY: *Normal People*

TURN-ONS: Intellectual connections, weird girls

TURN-OFFS: Being mocked by his peers

Luckily for you, this popular jock doesn't just go for the cute girls everyone else has crushes on. He's up for a secret fling with the young woman his friends at school make fun of, even if he feels kind of weird about it. Just watch out if you have insecurities linked to family trauma, because this guy is emotionally immature and a bit self-conscious about his social standing, and he might blow you off to take a more popular girl to the dance.

While this hunky young adult may not give you the happily ever after you crave, if you're looking for a slow-burn, on-again, off-again situationship with a guy from your past that spans your college years and accompanies your experiences of success, mistreatment, and self-discovery, sensitive Connell just might be your man.

romance novels, or that romance novels have a lot in common with Jane Austen. And I think books in *any* genre have the capacity to be sociopolitically subversive. But anything popular also has the ability to reinforce the status quo, sometimes even *while* subverting it—and, as we'll see when we discuss the history of the Gothic, popular literature has a track record of doing just that. I am not suggesting you should stop reading romance novels and I don't think romance novels are more effective at propping up the patriarchy than, say, literary fiction or experimental film. I also recognize that genre is and always has been linked to gender, and acknowledge that criticizing romance novels (which I'm not doing!) along feminist lines can also mean functionally critiquing femininity or femme identity.

All that said, I think it's worth asking why so much romance literature (of all brow heights) kind of feels like *Pride and Prejudice* fan fiction. How has the character of Darcy—a man who seems like a jerk but turns out to be your soulmate once he makes amends for his mistakes and reveals his true self to you—become the template for such a huge number of romantic heroes? What work is the Darcy trope doing, and might it also be doing some real damage?

Here's *Pride and Prejudice* in a nutshell. (Mr. Collins and Mary are sitting in a corner of the nutshell, having a deep conversation about the philosophical merits of the nutshell metaphor.) A hottie with a body (of wealth), Charles Bingley, rents an estate in the British countryside. He's moving in a group that includes his sisters, his brother-in-law, and his best bro, Fitzwilliam Darcy. The estate he rents is close to Netherfield, the estate where the Bennets live with their five daughters. Mrs. Bennet is desperate to get her daughters married, as the estate will pass to a distant male heir, the obsequious Mr. Collins, after her husband dies, meaning that she and her daughters will be left to depend on the kindness of their community for their basic necessities, including shelter.

Elizabeth "Lizzy" Bennet, the second oldest Bennet sister, has a chance encounter with Darcy at a ball, during which he insults her. During that same ball, Bingley and Lizzy's older sister, Jane, start crushing hard on each other, enough so that when Bingley's sisters invite Jane to visit, Mrs. Bennet sends her on horseback, hoping this will result in an extended stay that might precipitate a proposal. Indeed, Jane gets caught in the rain and becomes ill, causing her to get stuck at Bingley's estate and leading Lizzy to trek over in the mud to care for her.

Thrown together at Bingley's estate, Darcy and Lizzy commence a slow-burn will-they-won't-they. Over the course of the novel, they will need to overcome a series of obstacles to be together: his pride, her prejudice against him, their initial impressions of each other (Austen's original title for the story was *First Impressions*), Darcy's decision to separate Bingley and Jane, and the dark rumors about Darcy spread by his childhood friend and adulthood nemesis, George Wickham, a serial predator who is after sex and money.

As Lizzy learns to love Darcy, the reader learns to love him, too. Literary scholar Kathleen Lubey tells me that, when she teaches *Pride and Prejudice*, she makes fun of herself for loving Darcy, showing clips from the movie adaptations and fanning herself when the character comes on-screen. She asks her students to think about how the novel turns them into "desiring beings"—that is, how it asks them to want Darcy, or at least someone similar. Lubey goes on to explain that, historically speaking, any marriage in nineteenth-century England was one in which women were relatively powerless. So, what does it mean that Austen makes her readers want that?

Regardless of the problems with nineteenth-century marriage, Austen's marriage plot sells us on the idea of a love match. Darcy admires and desires Lizzy enough to change for her, or, at least, enough to make amends for past decisions that hurt her and those she loves. In what is probably his ultimate grand gesture, Darcy pays his nemesis, Wickham, to marry Lizzy's youngest sister, Lydia, whom Wickham has seduced and who refuses to leave him. Darcy's solution to this problem is a deeply problematic act in itself, as we'll discuss, but it does involve overcoming his pride and past trauma (Wickham had previously attempted to elope with Darcy's sister, and squandered the money Darcy gave him after their fathers died). Darcy says that in doing this, he thought only of Elizabeth, which is admittedly hot as hell.

Herein lies the Darcy myth: the fantasy that the person who at first seems arrogant and insulting will in fact become your soulmate once you put in the work, and might in fact ultimately be more of a catch because you had to convince them. Within the narrow archetype of his relationship with Lizzy, Darcy presents a romantic ideal that is a bit of a double-edged sword. First, while everyone else thinks Darcy is a jerk and that Lizzy dislikes him, she comes to know the truth: that he is good, and kind, and doesn't deserve his bad reputation. The idea that everyone villainizes your crush because they just don't know or understand him the way that you do is, for fairly obvious reasons, a dangerous and nonreplicable trope. Second, and this is crucial for understanding Jane Austen's outsize influence on the romance genre, Darcy attempts to make amends, acknowledges his mistakes (sort of), and makes things right where he was wrong, all while resolving past trauma that gets more made more explicit in later iterations of the romance genre. (If *Pride and Prejudice* came out of the *Bridgerton* writers' room today, we'd probably get a lot more background about Darcy's relationship with his father and the tensions among Darcy, Wickham, and Darcy's sister growing up.)

The Darcy fantasy provides cover for predatory behavior on multiple fronts. First, within the world of the novel, Darcy's act of chaining Lydia to her predator—or, to put a more positive spin on things, of paying Lydia's lover so that he can afford to marry her—means that Wickham never has to take the fall for his bad behavior. In the process of solving his own marriage plot, proving his righteousness, forging the love marriage his tremendous privilege affords him, bridging the social gap between his aristocratic position and Lizzy's more complicated status as a respectable but broke gentleman's daughter, or whatever other virtuous things he thinks he's doing, Darcy throws money at the villain of the story to make things right. In so doing, he provides cover for toxic, predatory behavior. By stepping in and taking care of Lizzy, Jane, and Lydia's problems as a father might, Darcy functions as a figurative patriarch. Along the way, he props up a social system in which Wickham, at least to a certain extent, gets away with his toxicity.

In the broader world, the Darcy figure provides cover for predatory behavior because we get sold this myth—a myth that has had an outsize influence on romance, romantic comedy, and the tropes that define our shared notions of love more generally. This myth trains us to view a potential partner's red flags as green lights, a dangerous prospect indeed.

To get to the heart of why the Darcy figure is so dangerous, in the chapters that follow we'll see how Jane Austen's fiction was influenced not only by the social structures of her time but also by the Gothic terror novels she liked to read. Gothic novels— propulsive page-turners that often strand their heroines in places haunted by the sins of the past, if not by literal ghosts—simultaneously offered an escape from and a commentary on the real world, which has always been dangerous for women. Much like contemporary romance, Gothic novels were self-consciously geared toward a largely female readership; from a sociopolitical perspective, these stories were often subversive but not particularly progressive. So, for example, a Gothic novel might comment on the patriarchy by dropping its heroine in a haunted abbey where an evil man is trying to entrap her—but when she escapes, she's still going to encounter her knight in shining armor. Like the heroines of Gothic novels, Austen's heroines often (but not always) experience some precarity and then resolve that tension by getting married and stepping into their roles upholding the existing social structure as wives and mothers.

When we read Austen in relation to and in the context of the Gothic, we are reminded of what we already know: that not every woman in the story can make it out alive. It might be worth asking, then, how the Darcy myth mixes fears and warnings with its romantic fantasy, and what might change if we read Austen with the goal of uncovering these fears and warnings.

Before we go any further, I want to talk about gender for a moment. Jane Austen wrote in a deeply heteronormative, patriarchal time, and the persistent cultural work of the Darcy myth is, in large part, to uphold patriarchal structures and excuse toxic masculinity. For this reason, while the Darcy myth is prominent enough in contemporary culture to influence us all, heterosexual women and anyone raised and socialized as a woman, period, might be particularly prone to having internalized its messages. That said, in Austen's age and in our own, Darcys proliferate across gender and other identity markers, as dominant cultural tropes influence all kinds of people and relationships.

We should also note that, in eighteenth- and nineteenth-century England, there were people who today would likely identify as gay and asexual and trans and nonbinary. While Austen moved in fairly conservative circles, it is fair to assume that she had some awareness of the gender and sexual diversity that has always existed; indeed, scholars have crafted compelling queer readings of some of the relationships in Austen's books. I won't be getting into these in detail in this book, but situating Austen's fiction within the history of the Gothic means linking it to a literary tradition deeply invested in transgressive notions of gender and sexuality. And historical literary figures broke with societal expectations not only on the page but also in real life. For example, Mary Shelley, the author of *Frankenstein*, helped her friends Walter Sholto Douglas and Isabella Robinson—a trans man and his partner—get false passports and travel to Paris as husband and wife. We can link this moment of microcosmic but telling activism, and Shelley's approach to gender in general, to the work of her mother (and feminism's foremother), Mary Wollstonecraft, which was deeply influential to Shelley's thinking about what it means to be a person in the world. In the pages that follow, I'll touch on Wollstonecraft's own contribution to the Gothic genre, an unfinished novel that can help us think about the starkness and darkness lurking in the margins of Austen's literary confections. In other words, "women's writing" is always a slippery and expansive category, and there is no mythic history of Western feminism without trans liberation.

All of this is to say that this book is for you, whoever you are. When I talk about women, I'm talking about how these stories or social structures think of women, but it may resonate with you no matter your gender. Darcys come in all shades and stripes, and my goal is to untangle this mythology so that we—all of us and any of us!—can liberate our desires and use our energy for our own purposes instead of to prop up boring, toxic expectations. Feminism should support the liberation of *everyone* toward *collective* good, and I hope this little book can take one small step in that direction by revealing how we have been bamboozled by our book boyfriend for generations.

Because while there is a lot to love about Darcy, there is much to fear in the Darcy myth, and coming to terms with Austen's influence on our thinking about love and romance will go a long way toward recognizing where the Darcy myth stops and our real lives begin.

I asked the participants in my recent Jane Austen seminar—a group of college students born between the years 1999 and 2002—to share their relationships with the figure of Mr. Darcy. The class was composed primarily of English majors, but not everyone had read Austen before. At this point in the quarter, I had asked them to read the first third of *Pride and Prejudice.*

One student, Lyza, who had neither finished the book nor seen the movies, reported, "We've all seen the screenshots. I knew that they would eventually get together, right? I knew that he was a controversial figure, so I knew that it was a slow burn, but I didn't know that it was an enemies-to-lovers plot. So I'm obsessed." The student sitting next to Lyza, Irving, built on these sentiments: "I just knew that people felt quite strongly about Mr. Darcy, in one of a couple of directions. I knew that the character was pretty polarizing and that some people thought he was like this closed-off romantic type. Some people thought he was a douche. It kind of goes one or the other way and I get why now, because that's what the whole story is about so far." Other students followed, calling Darcy mean, rude, socially incompetent, and "not awesome." CJ told us that his mom used to play one of the movie adaptations of *Pride and Prejudice* in the background while she was cooking. He never paid much attention to it, but he knew that Darcy was supposed to fix his errors through love, and CJ was hoping that would play out well.

The students talked about how their friends date people who don't treat them well, about the fun of the chase, about not wanting love to feel too easy. About dangerous lessons, in girlhood, about the bad boy who is good for you. About endorphins and adrenaline, banter that turns into flirtation, being interested in the person you can't have, liking the person you were planning to ghost just because they ghosted you first. I asked, why? Why would you like someone better once they've ghosted you? They said, because of Darcy. They said, for the same reason you want Chick-fil-A on Sundays when it's closed: because your brain wants what you can't have. They said, because you want to be wanted.

Am I blaming all of our dysfunctions about romance on Darcy? Obviously not. But do I think that Darcy has played a role here? I absolutely do. Look, literary history is full of guys you wouldn't want your best friend to date. Some of these guys are heroes. (I'm looking at you, Odysseus.) Some of them are disrespectful, or downright cruel. (Billy Shakespeare's *Taming of the* What Now?) Jane Austen didn't invent the slow-burn enemies-to-lovers plot and she's not totally responsible for the dangerous messages it perpetuates. And yet, I would venture to say that none of these literary figures have a hold on our shared ideas about dreamboats *quite* as strong as Mr. Darcy's. Even if another bookish bad boy springs to mind for you, if we're ready to undo the damage literature has wrought on our relationships, *Pride and Prejudice* is as good a place as any to start. This book is my attempt to hold Darcy accountable for his cultural legacies, and to hold us all accountable for what we have made of him. To ask what it would mean to love Darcy while releasing our hold on the Darcy myth.

2

TL;DR:
PRIDE AND PREJUDICE

*M*aybe you've read *Pride and Prejudice* nine million times, like I have, or even more times than that. Maybe you've never been able to get into it. Maybe you read it a long time ago, or you've only seen the films. Maybe Jane Austen is new to you altogether.

In any case, if we are going to discover a dark, radical reading of one of the most famous love stories of all time, then we need to get on the same page (literally). With that in mind, buckle up and join me for a quick *Pride and Prejudice* refresher course. (If you have the novel memorized, you can probably skip this chapter, although if you have *Pride and Prejudice* memorized, I bet you aren't a chapter-skipper.)

Volume I

"It is a truth universally acknowledged, that a single man in possession of a good fortune, must be in want of a wife." So begins Jane Austen's famous love story, *Pride and Prejudice*, which she once described in a letter to her sister as "rather too light, and bright, and sparkling." (As we'll see, Austen preferred things to be a little dark—which *Pride and Prejudice* definitely is, even if it's sparkling too!) With this famous opening line, Austen introduces us to the whisper networks that govern public opinion in the novel. (More specifically, Austen's canny **NARRATOR**, the constructed persona who is able to move into and out of various characters' perspectives, introduces us to these networks.) Right away, Austen reminds us that for privileged, white families in Regency England, cash is key and can easily be exchanged for love. Marriage is a financial proposition.

That marriage is a financial proposition is very good news to the socially ham-handed **MRS. BENNET**, because she finds herself in a difficult position. Her husband, **MR. BENNET**, thinks that both she and most of their five daughters are airheads, but Mrs. Bennet knows that they are also desperate. "Mr. Bennet's property consisted almost entirely in an estate of two thousand a year, which, unfortunately for his daughters, was entailed in default of heirs male, on a distant relation." This means that, when Mr. Bennet dies, this distant relation, the pompous and obsequious **MR. COLLINS**, will inherit **LONGBOURN** (the name of the estate) and be able to turn Mr. Bennet's surviving family out of the house as soon as he pleases. In other words, unless the Bennet sisters are able to marry well, they're screwed, and will be left with their mother's small inheritance and the kindness and pity of their community to protect and keep them.

Nerd Note: Using a third-person narrator who can inhabit the perspectives of each character in turn, letting us know what they thought as well as what they did, is known among scholars as *free indirect discourse*. Austen didn't invent this literary technique, but she's widely considered to have perfected it.

There are five Bennet sisters in all. The eldest, beautiful, mild-mannered **JANE**, sees the best in everybody. The second oldest, our charming heroine **ELIZABETH**, or **LIZZY**, doesn't take herself too seriously. Middle child **MARY** is a geek who buries herself in her studies, while the youngest daughters, **KITTY** and **LYDIA**, are obsessed with clothes, balls, gossip, and soldiers. Rather than keeping the youngest daughters at home while the eldest go husband hunting, the sisters are all "out," meaning they all get to go have fun at balls and such, and they are all also expected to be on the prowl for husbands.

So it's good news indeed when **CHARLES BINGLEY** rents **NETHER-FIELD PARK**, a nearby estate. Despite teasing his wife and daughters about it, Mr. Bennet is among the first of Bingley's new neighbors to pay him a visit, and the Bennet sisters soon see him at a ball, which he attends with his two sisters, his brother-in-law, and "another young man."

This young man is **MR. DARCY**, and he quickly makes a series of impressions on the community. (Remember those whisper networks I mentioned above?) Darcy is first noticed for his "fine, tall person, handsome features, noble mien; and the report which was in general circulation within five minutes after his entrance, of his having ten thousand a year." While those in attendance at the ball are quite taken with him at first, halfway through the evening "his manners gave a disgust which turned the tide of his popularity; for he was discovered to be proud, to be above his company, and above being pleased; and not all his large estate in Derbyshire could then save him from having a most forbidding, disagreeable countenance, and being unworthy to be compared with his friend." With this change in the social tides, Darcy's character goes from rich hottie to pompous jerk faster than you can ask, "Who's the new guy?"

Somehow, despite being socially awkward as fuck and never actually speaking to her directly, Darcy manages to insult Lizzy, who, according to her dad, "has something more of quickness than her sisters." There are more women than men at the ball, and so Lizzy has been sitting down instead of dancing when Darcy and Bingley have a conversation within earshot.

"Come, Darcy," Bingley says, "I must have you dance. I hate to see you standing about by yourself in this stupid manner. You had much better dance."

Darcy rejects this suggestion. He replies, "I certainly shall not. You know how I detest it, unless I am particularly acquainted with my partner. At such an assembly as this, it would be insupportable. Your sisters are engaged, and there is not another woman in the room, whom it would not be a punishment to me to stand up with."

A punishment! Within earshot of our quick little Lizzy!

Bingley, however, has been having a great time at the ball, and is already crushing hard on Jane Bennet. His reply expresses his in-

Meet a Darcy

NAME: Fitzwilliam Darcy

LOVE STORY: *Pride and Prejudice*

TURN-ONS: Intelligence, beautiful eyes, a light and pleasing form, easy playfulness

TURN-OFFS: Impropriety, triviality, making new friends

He is rude to you and insults you the moment he sees you. He snubs your family and convinces his best bro to ghost your sister. He seems like he's just not that into you, but actually he's super into you, he just has a funny way of showing it. If you have the self-confidence, patience, and self-assuredness to tangle with this tall, awkward rich kid, then Fitzwilliam Darcy might be the heartthrob for you!

A fun fact about our funky friend Fitzwilliam? He's a fixer. (He may be a bit of a fixer-upper too, but we know you're up for the challenge.) When Fitzy makes a mistake, he makes things right, and when someone in your life makes a mistake, you can bet on this handsome hunk to swoop in and help.

Pass up the chance to hang out with darling Darcy, and the mistake might be your own! But don't worry. This honey is generous when it comes to giving people second chances . . . well, at least when it comes to you, that is.

dignation. "I would not be so fastidious as you are," he cries, "for a kingdom! Upon my honour, I never met with so many pleasant girls in my life, as I have this evening; and there are several of them you see uncommonly pretty."

In response to this, Darcy calls Jane Bennet "the only handsome girl in the room," to which Bingley replies that Jane is, indeed, "the most beautiful creature" he "ever beheld." But then Bingley points out how pretty Elizabeth is and offers to ask Jane to make an introduction between Darcy and Lizzy.

And then Darcy—oh, Darcy—turns around to see who Bingley means. He looks at Elizabeth until their eyes meet, then pulls his gaze away and says coldly, "She is tolerable; but not handsome enough to tempt *me*, and I am in no humour at present to give consequence to young ladies who are slighted by other men. You had better return to your partner and enjoy her smiles, for you are wasting your time with me." Lizzy is insulted, of course, but she also has a "lively, playful disposition," and delights in anything ridiculous, and so she tells this story to her friends with "great spirit."

That night, it becomes clear to Lizzy that her sister Jane really does like Mr. Bingley. Jane's crush and her generous nature also lead her to like Bingley's sisters, **CAROLINE**, who is after Darcy, and **LOUISA**, who is married. Lizzy herself can easily see that Bingley's sisters are stuck-up and selfish.

In the days that follow, the Bennet sisters and their mother discuss the ball among themselves and with their close friends, the Lucas family, who live nearby. The eldest sister in that family, **CHARLOTTE**, is Elizabeth's good friend. The Bennet ladies also pay a visit to Bingley's sisters. Lizzy begins to fear that Jane is being too subtle about her affection for Bingley, and discusses this with Charlotte, who shares her concern, mentioning that Bingley does not know Jane's disposition and will need her encouragement to fall in love.

While she's focused on Jane and Bingley's interactions, Lizzy doesn't notice that Mr. Darcy is beginning to admire her.

Mr. Darcy had at first scarcely allowed her to be pretty; he had looked at her without admiration at the ball; and when they next met, he looked at her only to criticize. But no sooner had he made it clear to himself and his friends that she had hardly a good feature in her face, than he began to find it was rendered uncommonly intelligent by the beautiful expression of her dark eyes. To this discovery succeeded some others equally mortifying. Though he had detected with a critical eye more than one failure of perfect symmetry in her form, he was forced to acknowledge her figure to be light and pleasing; and in spite of his asserting that her manners were not those of the fashionable world, he was caught by their easy playfulness.

Lizzy is totally oblivious to his feelings: "to her he was only the man who made himself agreeable no where, and who had not thought her handsome enough to dance with." At one point, showing a certain obliviousness himself, Darcy mentions Lizzy's "fine eyes" to Caroline (come on, man!), opening himself up to all kinds of jealous teasing from that quarter.

A militia regiment arrives in the nearby village of Meryton, giving Kitty and Lydia an object for their attentions. They talk about officers all the time, and their father declares them "two of the silliest girls in the country."

Caroline and Louisa invite Jane to visit Netherfield. Since it looks like it will rain, Mrs. Bennet insists that Jane go on horseback in hopes that she will need to stay overnight. Jane does indeed get caught in the rain, and wakes up feeling ill. Mr. Bennet teases his wife, saying "if your daughter should have a dangerous fit of illness, if she should die, it would be a comfort to know that it was all in pursuit of Mr. Bingley, and under your orders." The news of Jane's illness worries Lizzy, so she decides to go take care of her, walking with Kitty and Lydia as far as Meryton and then continuing on her own, getting muddy in the process. Caroline and Louisa are totally taken aback; it strikes them as completely uncouth that Lizzy came on foot, walked by herself, and dirtied her clothes in the mud. Later, competitive Caroline, who wants Darcy for herself, criticizes Lizzy to him, scoffing at her "abominable sort of conceited independence, a most country town indifference to decorum." Darcy makes the mistake of mentioning that Lizzy's eyes "were brightened by the exercise," and RIP Caroline Bingley. Lizzy ends up staying at Netherfield to care for Jane and assist in her recovery, which means that she and Darcy get to advance their slow burn with lots of witty banter. She's not feeling him yet, but he is certainly into her. Austen tells us that Darcy "really believed, that were it not for the inferiority of her connections, he should be in some danger." At one point, after Darcy and Lizzy have had one of their delicious little back-and-forths, Darcy begins "to feel the danger of paying Elizabeth too much attention."

Nerd Note: The use of the word *danger* is interesting here. Darcy is extremely wealthy and can marry whoever he chooses, so the danger of marrying beneath him (socially and financially) is really just danger to his brand. By contrast, the Bennet sisters need to marry well in order to have a place to live and food on the table. Nonetheless, Lizzy doesn't seem too worried, and is able to take things as they come—even if that means she has an unexpected new frenemy in Caroline Bingley.

Mr. Collins arrives to Longbourn with the intention of marrying one of the Bennet sisters, thus tying the girls back to their home. Despite this altruistic intention, he is totally unappealing, pompous to the point of ridiculousness, and all but obsessed with his wealthy patroness, **LADY CATHERINE DE BOURGH**, who also happens to be Mr. Darcy's overbearing aunt. Considering Jane to be nearly engaged to Bingley, Mrs. Bennet directs Mr. Collins toward Lizzy, who is "equally next to Jane in birth and beauty." (While social expectation might dictate that Lizzy should marry before her younger sisters, let's take a moment to suggest that bookish, self-important Mary would probably have been happy to marry Mr. Collins, and was robbed.) When Mr. Collins eventually proposes to Lizzy, she rejects him, inciting her mother's fury and her father's approbation. In response to the ensuing uproar, Mr. Bennet tells Lizzy that "From this day you must be a stranger to one of your parents.—Your mother will never see you again if you do not marry Mr. Collins, and I will never see you again if you do." Lizzy responds with a smile. Mr. Collins ends up marrying Lizzy's friend Charlotte, who draws his attentions to herself and accepts his offer, thus settling for a marriage of convenience rather than "dying an old maid" and becoming a burden to her family. This pragmatic decision creates some tension between Charlotte and Elizabeth.

During this same period, the Bennet ladies make the acquaintance of a dashing young man who Elizabeth finds particularly appealing. This is the handsome and charming Mr. Wickham, who has just joined the regiment stationed at Meryton, and who has "the best part of beauty, a fine countenance, a good figure, and very pleasing address"—a pretty boy who has a way with words. From the first moment of Wickham's introduction, it is clear that he and Darcy have a history. When they first cross paths, they're astonished to see each other—"one looked white, the other red"—and Lizzy's right there to watch the awkwardness unfold. In her ensuing meetings with Wickham, Lizzy finds him more than willing to satisfy her curiosity and, given his charm, doesn't realize that he's a pathological liar. Wickham tells Lizzy that Darcy's father, his godfather, left him a position in the church that came with a significant annual income, but that Darcy chose not to honor his father's intentions, instead giving the position to another man. Wickham claims that Darcy hates him, but that he won't bad-mouth Darcy out of loyalty to Darcy's father (although he is of course bad-mouthing him, and will continue to do so). Wickham blames Darcy's actions toward him on jealousy and competition for the late Mr. Darcy's affections, calls Darcy's sister prideful and says that "she is nothing to me now," and also tells Lizzy that Darcy is set to marry Lady Catherine de Bourgh's sickly daughter, **ANNE**, thereby consolidating the family's wealth and uniting the two estates. Wickham doesn't show his face at the next ball; Lizzy dances with Darcy and makes barbed comments about Wickham, and, firmly in the enemy phase of their enemies-to-lovers storyline, their conversation has a certain frisson. Whatever sexual tension is building is however hampered, somewhat, by the embarrassing behavior of Elizabeth's relatives.

Suddenly, things take a turn. Jane receives a note from Caroline saying that their whole party has left Netherfield without any intention of coming back. Lizzy thinks Caroline wants her brother to marry Darcy's sister, **GEORGIANNA**, and insists to Jane that "No one who has ever seen you together, can doubt his affection." Kind, sweet Jane gives Caroline the benefit of the doubt, and, following Lizzy's encouragement, is "gradually led to hope . . . that Bingley would return to Netherfield and answer every wish of her heart."

Volume II

Caroline writes again, confirming that the party is settled in London and including Bingley's regret at not having had time to say goodbye. Jane is heartbroken, and Lizzy is pissed. Mrs. Bennet, naturally, is beside herself, while Mr. Bennet continues not to take anything seriously. "So, Lizzy," he says one day, "your sister is crossed in love I find. I congratulate her. Next to being married, a girl likes to be crossed in love a little now and then. . . . Let Wickham be *your* man. He is a pleasant fellow, and would jilt you creditably." Lizzy has more patience with her dad than I do, and plays along with the joke. Liberated by Darcy's departure, Wickham talks shit about him even more blatantly than before, "and every body was pleased to think how much they had always disliked Mr. Darcy before they had known any thing of the matter."

Mrs. Bennet's brother and his wife, **MR. AND MRS. GARDINER**, come for Christmas. They are sensible, kind tradespeople with whom Lizzy is on intimate terms. Mrs. Gardiner takes it upon herself to warn Lizzy against falling in love with Wickham, who has no fortune, and Lizzy replies that she will do her best. Wickham soon redirects his attentions toward a girl who has come into some money. Mr. and Mrs. Gardiner take Jane back to London with them, and she waits for a visit from her friends, but is largely ignored until finally Caroline stops by. The visit is brief and cold, and Jane is hurt by the party's desertion of her and by this sudden change in Caroline's behavior.

A couple of months later, Lizzy goes to visit Charlotte in her new home and is contented to find her friend in a comfortable situation. During the visit, Lizzy gets to know pompous, hypercritical Lady Catherine de Bourgh, who finds fault with Lizzy's upbringing. Lizzy argues back politely, and Lady Catherine is a bit scandalized.

Later in Lizzy's visit, Mr. Darcy and his cousin, **COLONEL FITZWILLIAM**, arrive. There is more rising sexual tension between Elizabeth and Darcy, and more witty banter, and more will-they-won't-they, and more Darcy awkwardness. Then, one day, Darcy shows up at Charlotte's house and finds Lizzy alone. Charlotte returns, interrupting their visit; when Darcy departs, she tells Lizzy, "he must be in love with you, or he would never have called on us in this familiar way." Charlotte starts paying attention to Darcy and trying to get to the bottom of his feelings, but he is inscrutable. Lizzy starts bumping into Mr. Darcy on her walks and walking with him in awkward silence and stilted conversation. She wonders why this keeps happening.

Then Lizzy has a conversation with Colonel Fitzwilliam in which he lets slip that Mr. Darcy "congratulated himself on having lately saved a friend from the inconveniences of a most imprudent marriage" based on some "strong objections against the lady." Lizzy understands immediately that Darcy has been the cause of her sister's pain. Lizzy is livid to the point of headache, stays back when the rest of the party convenes that evening, and rereads Jane's letters, feeling that "Mr. Darcy's shameful boast of what misery he had been able to inflict, gave her a keener sense of her sister's suffering."

And then suddenly Darcy is there. He is there, and he has come to declare his love and propose. Elizabeth is astonished, and then increasingly angry, as Darcy goes on to detail "his sense of her inferiority—of its being a degradation—of the family obstacles which judgment had always opposed to inclination." Elizabeth turns him down, surprising him. He asks her why "with so little *endeavor* at civility" he has been rejected. Meeting his anger and passion, Lizzy asks why his proposal was so insulting, and tells him that she could never "accept the man, who has been the means of ruining, perhaps for ever, the happiness of a most beloved sister." She asks if Darcy denies separating Bingley and Jane, and Darcy replies, "I have no wish of denying that I did every thing in my power to separate my friend from your sister, or that I rejoice in my success. Towards *him* I have been kinder than towards myself." Lizzy brings up Wickham, and Darcy scoffs, thanking her for explaining her opinion so fully. Growing more enraged, Lizzy tells him that she has thought of him as arrogant, conceited, and selfish since their very first meeting, and concludes, "I had not known you a month before I felt that you were the last man in the world whom I could ever be prevailed on to marry." Darcy departs, leaving her in a tumult; the next morning, he finds her on her walk and presses a letter into her hand.

Darcy's letter is not an apology, but it is an explanation. He explains that he was not convinced that Jane returned Bingley's affections, and his objection to the marriage was heightened by the "total want of propriety" displayed by Lizzy's mother, younger sisters, and sometimes father. Darcy does not regret separating the two lovebirds, but does feel some regret for concealing Jane's presence in London from Bingley.

The heart of Darcy's letter, however, is his explanation of his relationship with Wickham. Wickham, he tells Lizzy, was the son of the man who managed Darcy's father's estates, and was also Darcy's father's godson. Darcy's father paid for Wickham's education and hoped that he would pursue the church as his profession. Following the deaths of both Darcy's and Wickham's fathers, Wickham told Darcy he did not want to join the clergy and instead planned to study law. He asked for money instead of a position, which Darcy gave him. Wickham went on to live "a life of idleness and dissipation." Eventually, finding himself in tough financial straits when the position that had been intended for him in the church became available, he changed his mind and told Darcy he wanted to be ordained. Darcy refused to comply with Wickham's wishes. But villains tend to resurface, and Wickham did exactly that. The previous summer, Darcy explains, his sister Georgianna went to a fashionable coastal town with a lady named **MRS. YOUNGE**, who had been hired to watch over her young charge but who in fact had a prior relationship with Wickham. Wickham followed them, and sweet-talked Georgianna into eloping with him, leaning on her fond feelings for him from when she was a child. Luckily, Georgianna told Darcy everything, because she was "unable to support the idea of grieving and offending a brother whom she almost looked up to as a father." She was thus able to avoid being tricked by Wickham, who was after her fortune and after revenge. Lizzy realizes, from Wickham's own words and actions, that what Darcy tells her must be true, and she is filled with shame.

Lizzy travels home, reuniting with her sisters. She decides to conceal from Jane any details that relate to her and might bring her pain, but otherwise tells her what transpired between Darcy and herself, and the truth about Wickham. Since Wickham's regiment will soon leave Meryton for the fashionable seaside town of Brighton, the sisters determine not to make his true character known—but they do not realize this is a mistake. Soon the wife of the colonel of the regiment invites Lydia to come along to Brighton, causing drama between Lydia and the envious Kitty. Lizzy thinks, rightly, that letting Lydia go to Brighton is a bad idea, but Mr. Bennet replies, "Lydia will never be easy till she has exposed herself in some public place or other, and we can never expect her to do it with so little expense or inconvenience to her family as under the present circumstances." Mr. Bennet goes on to claim, wrongly, that Lydia is "luckily too poor to be an object of prey to any body," as if wealth is the only thing women are preyed on for.

Lizzy leaves on a trip with her aunt and uncle, the Gardiners. Initially, they are supposed to go to the Lake District, but the plans shift, and they end up taking a trip to Darcy's neck of the woods instead. The Gardiners want to tour Mr. Darcy's estate, **PEMBERLEY**, and since they hear reports that Darcy's family is not there for the summer, the party decides to go.

Volume III

Darcy's estate is a sight to behold, and Lizzy feels "that to be mistress of Pemberley might be something!" To protect herself against "something like regret," she tells herself that she would not have been allowed to invite the Gardiners to visit her there, because they are tradespeople, therefore "new money," therefore gauche. (This turns out to be untrue, and when Lizzy and Darcy end up together, they stay closely acquainted with her uncle and aunt.) The housekeeper speaks warmly of Mr. Darcy and Georgianna, calling Darcy "the best landlord, and the best master . . . that ever lived," and Lizzy sees signs of what a good and devoted brother he is.

Then Darcy shows up unexpectedly, of course. He and Lizzy lock eyes, and they blush, and then Darcy comes over. Darcy makes Lizzy and the Gardiners feel welcome on his grounds, and Lizzy and Darcy begin to spend time together. Lizzy even gets to know Georgianna, who is not proud, as Wickham claimed, but only shy. Things are finally going well for our star-crossed lovers, and even Lizzy must admit that she "certainly did not hate him." It seems like even an uncomfortable visit from the Bingley sisters can't mess things up for them now.

But then, another twist! A twist in the form of a letter, this time from Jane, and bearing painful news. Lydia has run away with Wickham. At first Jane calls this an imprudent match, but gives Wickham the benefit of the doubt, assuming they will marry for love. A second letter, however, expresses that, "imprudent as a marriage between Mr. Wickham and our poor Lydia would be, we are now anxious to be assured it has taken place." If Lydia has had a sexual escapade with a man who will not marry her, then she has committed an act of social ruin that will have a drastic impact on both herself and her family. Lizzy tells Darcy what has transpired, expressing her fear: "*You* know him too well to doubt the rest. She has no money, no connections, nothing that can tempt him to—she is lost for ever." Lizzy regrets that she didn't tell Lydia "what he was," by which she means a predator and a monster. Mr. Bennet has gone to London to find her, and Mr. Gardiner is going to catch up. Admitting that the situation "is every way horrible," Lizzy departs.

Lizzy arrives home to find her family in a tumult. The note Lydia left upon her departure with Wickham makes clear that she thinks they will soon be married, but as far as everyone can tell, no marriage has taken place. Wickham is discovered to have gambling debts, and not to have any close connections who know where he might be. Mr. Bennet returns home and admits to Lizzy that she was right when she told him not to let Lydia go to Brighton. A letter arrives from their uncle, saying that he has found Lydia and Wickham and asking Mr. Bennet to secure a share of what little money he has to pass on to Lydia. It is clear that a large sum of money is in play, which has induced Wickham to agree to marry Lydia on these terms, but it is unclear how, and the family assumes Mr. Gardiner is to thank.

Lydia and Wickham get married and come to visit Longbourn. While local gossips are disappointed that Lydia was not forced into exile or prostitution, the whisper networks that be must be contented that "with such an husband, her misery was considered certain." While talking about her wedding, Lydia lets slip to Lizzy that Mr. Darcy was there. Lizzy writes to her aunt to ask what transpired, and Mrs. Gardiner replies, telling her that Darcy went to Georgianna's former governess, Mrs. Younge, to get news about Wickham's whereabouts, which he finally pulled from her via "bribery and corruption." Darcy saw first Wickham, then Lydia, and tried to "persuade her to quit her present disgraceful situation, and return to her friends as soon as they could be prevailed on to receive her, offering his assistance, as far as it would go." But Lydia, "absolutely resolved on remaining where she was," refused to leave Wickham, explaining that they would get married at some point. It became clear to Darcy that Wickham had never intended to marry Lydia at all. Wickham had been running away from his debts and had simply taken Lydia with him for sex and company; he still had every intention of "making his fortune by marriage" to someone else. Darcy and Wickham thus entered into negotiations, and Darcy ended up agreeing to pay off Wickham's debts and set him up financially, thus, essentially, allowing him to make his fortune by marrying Lydia rather than leaving her socially ruined.

And now, the novel moves swiftly toward its happily ever after. Mr. Darcy is on a mission to undo the damage he has caused. Bingley returns and proposes to Jane. She accepts, of course.

And then, a final surprise: Lady Catherine de Bourgh visits unexpectedly. She has come to make sure Lizzy is not planning to marry Mr. Darcy, and to make sure Lizzy knows that Mr. Darcy is set to marry her own daughter, Anne. Lizzy is evasive—she admits that she is not engaged to Darcy, but refuses to promise not to enter into such an engagement.

Finally, Lizzy and Darcy have a heart-to-heart. Lizzy thanks Darcy for his "unexampled kindness to my poor sister," meaning Lydia, and Darcy tells Lizzy that, in helping Lydia, "I thought only of *you*." He then tells Lizzy that his "affections and wishes are unchanged, but one word from you will silence me on this subject for ever." Of course, Lizzy tells him she has changed her mind, and Darcy admits that his aunt's frustration at failing to receive the desired promise from Lizzy taught him to hope that she might now love him. Darcy says that his previous behavior had been "unpardonable," and he tells Lizzy about the conversations between himself and Bingley that redirected his friend toward marrying Jane. The air cleared between them, Lizzy and Darcy fall into an easy, loving rapport. They marry and live happily ever after.

But, as we'll see in the next chapter, it's actually quite a lot darker than that.

3

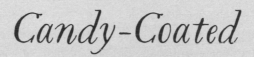

Candy-Coated

GOTHIC

or, Why Jane Austen Was
Actually Dark as Hell

*W*hile Jane Austen achieved only modest success and acclaim as a writer during her own time, her popularity has increased exponentially over the ensuing generations, and she is now widely regarded as a literary genius and cultural icon. Over the past two centuries, Austen's novels have been adapted in illustrations and theatrical productions, for film and TV, and across literary, internet, and pop-cultural genres. Austen has been adopted by some as a (proto)feminist political figure, and the amount of Austen merch is off the charts. There's an endless and ever-growing litany of *Pride and Prejudice* adaptations, and it's difficult to think of a woman writer who has become more of a cult figure than Jane Austen.

Maybe you can't stand Jane Austen—maybe you find the novels boring and the film adaptations overly saccharine and romantic. (And no shade if that's you.) But if you're one of the many fans who love her, there's a good chance you also *trust* her. As Austen scholar Deidre Lynch has argued, there is something "private and personal" about people's love of Austen, a general consensus that her novels make the reader feel *seen*. (In her recent book on the subject, Kathleen Anderson suggests that "the primary and quite simple reason that Jane Austen and her novels are so popular over two hundred years later, aside from their literary genius, is that she *likes* women.") Given the outsize popularity and influence of Austen's works, there's a good chance that, even if her books aren't your cup of tea, some of the media you consume is shaped by this sense of trust, as well.

But here's the problem: when we read Austen's work as romance that feels real, personal, and relatable, we get it wrong—or, at least, we miss out on a lot of the content and context. In so doing, we've made a dangerous mistake, because Jane Austen's works are actually *super* dark, cannily blending horror into the love stories they serve up. These tales and their hidden monsters have become indelibly linked to our ideas of romance, which means that, by getting Austen wrong, we've gotten romance wrong, too. Because, while Austen's heroines often get their happily ever after (a feature so important and familiar to romance fans that they simply refer to it as an HEA), they also illuminate the very real ways in which love is scary for women. And when we fail to heed their warnings, we throw ourselves into dangerous situations in the name of love.

Put another way, we can love Jane Austen, but we shouldn't always trust her.

When Austen first put pen to paper in the last decades of the eighteenth century, she built on a history of invention and innovation in British fiction, blending together different ideas of what a novel could be.

Early-eighteenth-century fiction hewed closely to reality, often taking the form of journals or letters and claiming to be found text. These books were didactic in nature, purporting to help readers find security and marriage while avoiding rakes—seductive gentlemen who would leave them socially ruined rather than married—and sexual assault.

The idea that fiction should include a teachable moment also had to do with the rise of children's literature. For example, the phrase *Goody Two-shoes* comes from an anonymous story published in London in 1765. In the story, a poor orphan with only one shoe has her virtue rewarded with a complete pair of shoes, a job as a teacher, and a wealthy husband.

Novels were assumed to reflect the real lives of women, and to help women navigate those lives. But the real lives of women back then were scary as hell. That showed up in novels too. One author, Eliza Haywood, wrote novels in which women reformed rakes, endured bad marriages, and even disguised themselves as strangers in order to seduce the same man multiple times. Across genres, Haywood registered the presence of violence and sexual violence in women's lives, treating it as a mundane reality. One heroine's perfectly respectable husband murders her pet in front of her, an act of cruelty her friend tells her is not enough abuse to justify a legal separation. Another heroine is raped at a masquerade when she mistakes someone for somebody else. When I discussed these grim moments with Haywood scholar Manushag Powell, this was her takeaway: "Haywood's point is: it doesn't matter how smart you are and how closely you follow the rules. You should still do that, obvs, but nothing will protect you from men. The question is more about how to tilt the odds than how to ensure a happy outcome. Because the answer for Haywood is never, like, go live in a nunnery or lock yourself in the basement. You have to go out and live life, knowing your life is dangerous."

Superstar novelist Frances Burney was no stranger to the pains of life as a woman—she even survived a mastectomy without anesthesia. In her 1778 work *Evelina, or the History of a Young Lady's Entrance into the World*, a young woman must take her rightful place as her father's heir and marry well while avoiding the advances of a rake, Sir Clement Willoughby, to whom Jane Austen's Willoughby (from *Sense and Sensibility*) might have been a tribute. Willoughby is constantly trapping Evelina—in his arms, in a dark alley, in his coach—and lavishing her with unwanted statements of affection under which the threat of real violence pulsates. To win at love, according to Burney, you have to recognize that love is a scary story.

Women writers weren't the only ones to acknowledge that the world was a dangerous place for women. Sexual assault and its aftermath served as a major theme for heavyweights like Samuel Richardson, whose 1748 doorstopper *Clarissa* could just as accurately be called *How to Die Gracefully in the Event of a Rape*.

But in the 1790s, a literary trend exploded in England, challenging didactic realism: the Gothic novel, also known as terror fiction or the terrorist system of novel writing. Scholars refer to this period as the "Gothic craze" or "Gothic explosion," because, in any given year, up to 38 percent of all published novels fell into the Gothic category. One influential publishing house, Minerva Press, churned out title after title, including the Northanger Horrid novels read by the characters in Jane Austen's *Northanger Abbey*. Publishing had hit upon a hot commodity, and readers were insatiable. Everybody— and I mean everybody—was reading terror fiction.

So, what makes a novel Gothic? Bursting from the shadowy, forbidden corners of earlier fiction, these novels abandoned country cottages and London social halls in favor of literal dungeons, shackles, and haunted abbeys. Gothic novels are marked by their settings—usually cavernous, ruined, and connected in some strange way to the past. The beautiful landscapes we tend to associate with more pastoral settings are often present in Gothic novels, too, with our heroines having special understanding of or access to the sublimity of the natural world. (Remember that scene in the 2005 *Pride and Prejudice* movie when Lizzy stands on a cliff, the wind in her skirt, piano music swelling around her? We zoom in on her face and she is all emotion and thought, the landscape outside mirroring the gorgeous landscape of her soul. That cinematic moment is the Gothic heroine in a nutshell—if she also did something like break out in poetry and then later play the lute.) In the world of the Gothic, ghosts, ghouls, devils, and monsters walk among the characters—or at least seem to. Secrets of the past, collective fears, and unspoken desires all linger in the atmosphere. Often, especially if a woman writer is holding the pen, there is a girl trapped in this dark world, and she must find her way out.

Literary historians sometimes make the mistake of reading these terrifying stories as something fresh and new—of assuming that, weary of tales that told them how to be and what to do, readers craved supernatural intrigue and a cool plunge into the collective unconscious. But when we look at the history of fiction written by women in England, we see that these scary stories built on their predecessors. It's not that monster narratives were suddenly more interesting than domestic tales, but that domestic tales were monster narratives in the first place. The real world has always been Gothic for women. Terror fiction gave authors a new way to express that truth.

Interestingly, subcategories of the Gothic genre were deeply influenced by questions of gender. The tension between horror and terror fiction is a case in point. One novelist of the time, Matthew "Monk" Lewis, who actually sounds like he was a sweet, chummy bro in person, wrote variations on the Gothic in which the main characters were ultimately consumed by the darkness and in which sexual and other violence was made explicit. Lewis's extremely disturbing novel *The Monk* exults in the depravity of violent acts; at the end of the book, we learn that the Devil himself has been pulling the strings. (I spoiled this one on purpose; don't read it.) Gothic tales like *The Monk* give the reader a safe space in which to indulge in the fantasy of doing horrible things. By contrast, protofeminist approaches to the Gothic invite the reader to cheer for, if not identify with, a heroine who must both escape from danger and restore the moral order. It was popular literary icon Ann Radcliffe—the Nora Roberts of her day—who called Lewis's work horror Gothic, as opposed to the terror Gothic she preferred. In Radcliffe's work, visions of the supernatural are quite literally the work of the patriarchy. Think Scooby-Doo: you see a ghost, sure, but there's some weird old rich guy pulling the strings. The fantasy of a terror Gothic book, then, lies in the vision of a woman claiming the power to recognize and reveal what has been concealed while setting things to rights (or inspiring her handsome suitor to do the same).

While of course not only women wrote—or read—terror fiction, the genre is deeply linked to women's subjectivity and the social pressures experienced by women in the period. Indeed, the protofeminist power of the Gothic novel was so great, even the pioneering women's rights advocate Mary Wollstonecraft tried her hand at the genre. While pregnant with her second daughter—the future

Mary Shelley, who would write that most famous of Gothic novels, *Frankenstein*—Wollstonecraft produced her most radical work of all, an unfinished novel that tackles topics including poverty, neglect, sexual assault, abortion, mental health, and the unjust systems that made it nearly impossible for women to divorce their husbands or secure access to their children following a separation. Before she could finish the novel Wollstonecraft suffered a terrible fate of her own. Shortly after she gave birth, a doctor with eighteenth-century ideas about hygiene reached into her body to remove her fragmented placenta, introducing an infection that would kill her. In Wollstonecraft's illness, she wasn't allowed to nurse her new baby—an act she had praised so boldly in her political philosophy—and puppies were brought in instead to draw off her milk. She died soon thereafter, leaving her daughters not with a mother but with an unfinished monster narrative—one that would haunt Mary Shelley for the rest of her life.

This shit is dark as fuck, and Jane Austen knew it.

Terror fiction was ubiquitous in Jane Austen's day and she totally loved it. We can see the depth of her engagement with the genre most directly in her first finished work, *Northanger Abbey*. In *Northanger Abbey*, the artless heroine, Catherine, both reads novels and thinks she's in a novel. Her comedic mistake is in assuming that her life will be as extra and dramatic as the books she reads. She's disappointed when her crush's estate, though called an "abbey," isn't spooky and ruined. She expects to find a skeleton or forbidden manuscript in a chest, but it's full of clean laundry. She even wonders if her crush's dad murdered his mom, and is quite embarrassed when her crush figures this out. The joke is on Catherine, however, because she's in the very Gothic *real* world—one in which her crush's dad, upon discovering Catherine isn't as rich as he'd thought, sends her home unattended and unprotected, thus leaving her open to both social and physical danger.

In *Northanger Abbey*, when we glimpse Catherine reading, Austen's chatty narrator defends this choice: "Alas! If the heroine of one novel be not patronized by the heroine of another, from whom can she expect protection and regard? I cannot approve of it. Let us leave it to the Reviewers to abuse such effusions of fancy at their leisure, and over every new novel to talk in threadbare strains of the trash with which the press now groans. Let us not desert one another; we are an injured body." The "injured body" here refers to both gender and genre—people don't respect Gothic novels, and don't respect the women who read them. But even though novels geared toward women are regarded as trash, women need one another—and need these stories—because they are acutely vulnerable to the threats of the world.

In addition to her tribute to terror fiction in *Northanger Abbey*, Austen's first writings are haunted by Gothic novels. In Austen's juvenilia, characters poison one another and kick each other out the window. In one early novella, *Lady Susan*, a monstrous mother steals her daughter's place on the marriage market. But while her most famous tales harken back to an earlier, less overblown moment in the history of literary fiction—one in which young ladies make their way in a novelization of the supposed real world—these stories are also infused with, even *haunted by*, the Gothic.

The drama of *Pride and Prejudice* hinges on the actions of a serial predator who targets young girls. So does the drama in *Sense and Sensibility*—one of the rake's victims, Eliza Williams, ends up a single mother and an outcast from polite society, while the other, heroine Marianne Dashwood, barely scrapes by, only because she never gets trapped by pregnancy (though I think there's enough evidence in the text to suggest that she does get pregnant, but manages to terminate). In class, I ask my students who has read *Sense and Sensibility*, and several people raise their hands. I ask them to keep their hand up if they remember Eliza Williams, and nobody does, because the women in Austen's fiction who meet Gothic fates disappear to make room for the marriage plot. In so doing, they become ghosts that haunt her canonical romances.

In another Austen novel, *Mansfield Park*, one of the characters is forever punished for a passionate affair with a seductive rake who broke her heart, then came calling once she'd settled for a marriage of convenience. The titular family home is haunted by the violence of colonial slave labor, which supports the family's folly from a distance. When we reread Austen through a Gothic lens, we see that threatening men, ruined women, and the everyday bloodshed of life under capitalist patriarchy haunt the margins of her love stories.

Look a little more closely and these love stories seem pretty dark, too. Even if we accept that Mr. Darcy's rude personality is of little consequence compared to his big heart (and even bigger house), and even if we believe that the nasty rumors about him aren't true, there is no denying that he pays a dangerous rake to marry our heroine's sister so that Darcy can marry Lizzy without tarnishing his reputation or sacrificing his brand. Told from Lydia's perspective, *Pride and Prejudice* is the story of a young heroine who is neglected, seduced, lied to, abducted, trapped, rejected, and ultimately chained to her predator. It's our beloved Darcy who locks her up.

How can we reconcile Darcy the hunk with Darcy the cruel, patriarchal enforcer? (Is it Darcy's fault these two categories are so difficult to distinguish in the first place?) Maybe we need to accept that Darcy contains multitudes. Because Mr. Darcy, much like Frankenstein's creature, is a strange amalgamation. In Mary Shelley's famous novel, she imagines a superhuman being sewn together from dead body parts by a college student who misunderstands what it means to make a friend. Scholars have noted that the creature's quilt-like structure is a metaphor for the novel as a whole, as Shelley stitches together genres including adventure story, Orientalist romance, and education narrative to produce her Gothic masterpiece. But *Pride and Prejudice* is stitched together too—informed both by more realistic storytelling styles and by terror fiction—and Darcy, much like Frankenstein's creature, is his own kind of monster, an assemblage of fears and desires, at once the villain and the heartthrob, the rescuer and the predator. He's a fascinating and confusingly appealing character, but he's in no way the ideal man.

How have we forgotten this?

Austen's Gothic sensibilities were misinterpreted as cozy romance almost right away—and generations of readers just went with it. An influential 1815 review of *Emma* commonly attributed to the famous novelist (and amateur dog breeder) Sir Walter Scott claimed that Austen had invented a new kind of fiction, one in which the author's "knowledge of the world" allowed her to present "characters that the reader cannot fail to recognize." The review argued that Austen's new take on fiction allowed her to create novels of real life—an approach to her work that has dominated popular reception to this day.

Even Austen herself has been understood as closely reflecting our real lives. In *The Making of Jane Austen*, which traces the rise of Austen fandom across generations, Devoney Looser argues that, from the family members who tried to secure Jane Austen's fame after her death to the illustrators who sensationalized her romances to the theater kids who adapted her works for the stage and the screen to the suffragists who claimed her as a feminist icon, "one near constant is that her imagined intimacy with audiences has been described as of the coziest, quotidian, familial kind." Austen fans, who sometimes embrace the title of Janeites, feel like they know both Austen and her characters, and have drawn inspiration from this sense of connection to form communities, create beautiful things, and even support political causes. Austen fandom has a long cultural history but includes some transhistorical trends. For example, according to Looser, we can trace contemporary Jane Austen fandom's attachment to the fabrics, flavors, and favorite spots of Austen's life to "the first decades of Austen's wide celebrity" in which Austen was widely known as "Aunt Jane."

But if Jane Austen is Aunt Jane and her characters remind us of people we know in real life, then we're going to read her novels as mirrors that reflect our everyday lives. And they do. It's just that when we interpret them as cozy realism, or comforting romance, we forget that they are also horror stories. We forget that they are also full of monsters.

We fall in love with these monsters. And, most dangerously, we hope they will love us back.

Quiz: Are YOU in a Gothic Novel?

Answer the following questions and keep track of how many As, Bs, and Cs you choose!

1. **WOULD YOU CONSIDER YOURSELF TO BE A HEROINE?**
   A. Alas! If I am born to be an heroine, I know it not. My parentage, my home, even my true name have remained, to this day, unknown to me.
   B. Girl, I think we *both* need to get in touch with our Big Main Character Energy.
   C. Sure, but I'm also the girl next door.

2. **ARE YOU TRAPPED IN A STATELY BUT CREEPY BUILDING, SUCH AS AN OLD MONASTERY IN THE WOODS OR THE *BACHELOR* MANSION?**
   A. Totes.
   B. I'm kinda trapped wherever I go, ya know?
   C. What, you mean like this estate that I'll get kicked out of the moment my father dies? When you put it that way, it's almost like my house is already haunted by my living father's ghost or something, lol.

3. **DO YOU EVER FEEL THAT HISTORY IS HAUNTING YOU?**
   A. You mean like that time I found a bloody dagger and a bundle of old letters in a secret chamber in the wall? Or more like the time I saw an actual ghost?

B. If I make one false move it'll haunt me for the rest of my life, that's for sure.

C. Maybe, but I prefer to ignore it.

4. HAVE YOU EVER MET A GHOST OR MONSTER IRL?

A. You would shudder if you could only imagine the horrors I have beheld!

B. I haven't seen anything supernatural, but I'm still afraid of the dark.

C. Do men and mothers count?

5. WHAT IS YOUR BIGGEST FEAR?

A. Corruption of the soul

B. Exile from society

C. Eh, I'll get my HEA. It's these *other* chicks who should worry.

RESULTS

MOSTLY A: Look out! You're in a scary story!

MOSTLY B: Whew, you're in a love story! Just don't mess it up because this could turn into a scary story really freakin' quickly!

MOSTLY C: You're in a Jane Austen novel, which looks like a love story but is secretly a scary story! Love is a dangerous game, and you'd better win.

4

Love Is a HAUNTED HOUSE

or, What *Pride and Prejudice* Would Look Like as a Horror Novel

We know (and Jane knew) that Austen's classic romances are deeply influenced by the Gothic, by the horror and terror of late-eighteenth-century popular fiction. Because Jane Austen is such an influential figure in the history of the novel, romance from Austen onward is thus infused with the Gothic—it is full of horror or, at least, callbacks to the Gothic genre and reminders that danger lurks in the shadows of our everyday lives and loves.

What happens, then, if we read *Pride and Prejudice* as a scary story?

Now, before I lose the Darcy lovers: I'm not necessarily claiming that *Pride and Prejudice* actually *is* a scary story, or that we need to read it that way all the time. Far be it from me to claim special knowledge of Jane Austen's intentions—that would be sacrilegious of me as an English professor! And there are, of course, important and satisfying takeaways that come when we read (and reread) *Pride and Prejudice* as a love story. Darcy shines as a romantic hero, and has become the basis for almost every romantic hero to follow, because he not only cuts a dashing figure but also recognizes and makes amends for his mistakes while resolving his past trauma, all in the service of forging an (at least emotionally) equal, consensual relationship with the smart girl. That's hot, and I get it.

And yet. Not every taciturn asshole is Darcy in disguise, or Darcy before he meets his match. Not every beast in a castle will give you an amazing library and transform into a prince if you're just, like, *persistent*. In other words, Darcy has given us some dangerous ideas. Whether you read *Pride and Prejudice* as ideal romance or as Gothic horror, it's important to reckon with how the Darcy blueprint has messed up our expectations of romantic prospects (especially men), from rude strangers at parties to emotionally withholding partners—all while generally twisting our ideas about love. (Real quick: it's not your job to fix anybody, and rude people at parties are often just jerks.) So whether you're a goth ready to paint Pemberley black or a tried-and-true Jane Austen aficionado deeply resistant to the idea that *Pride and Prejudice* might offer anything other than just deserts and a sweet resolution, excavating the novel for its hidden darkness is an important exercise because it helps us uncover what is harmful about our shared ideas of romance.

Because in Jane Austen's era—and in *Pride and Prejudice*—love is unquestionably scary for women. And by reading *Pride and Prejudice* for the danger that lurks at its margins, we can begin to understand what the danger in Austen's classic means for us today.

To understand *Pride and Prejudice* as a scary story, we're going to need to adjust our expectations. When we go in looking for an idealized marriage plot, the novel certainly delivers, because the genre contract formed between romance readers and romance authors is, in large part, derived from *Pride and Prejudice*. Whether or not you've read *Pride and Prejudice* before, if you've read or watched romance or romantic comedies, you've basically been trained to read it, and to pick up what it is (ostensibly) putting down. There's the apparent bad boy who actually turns out to be a loyal and loving (and wealthy) hottie; the smart, relatable heroine who turns him down when he doesn't yet deserve her; the slutty other woman who ends up with the sniveling jerk. The beautiful female friendship between Elizabeth Bennet and her sister Jane—which is probably a tribute to Jane Austen's feelings about her own dear sister, Cassandra—functions as a restorative force that overcomes the bad and misguided behaviors of others and leads the sisters to happily ever after with the men of their choosing. In other words, if you've enjoyed any of the interrelated genres that take *Pride and Prejudice* as their touchstone, you are definitely going to like this book (or, at least, one of the many film adaptations).

But what happens if you come to *Pride and Prejudice* with another set of genre conventions in mind? By looking at *Pride and Prejudice* through the lens of horror tropes, we can begin to reveal its Gothic underbelly, and to notice the fear and danger that haunt the novel and its world.

Longbourn Is a Haunted House

From its opening pages, *Pride and Prejudice* is set in a haunted house—even though the specter that's haunting it has to do with a death that hasn't happened yet. Lizzy and her sisters are growing up in a home they will lose the moment their father dies. They'll also lose the income that comes with their property, meaning they'll be completely dependent on their friends and relatives for survival—unless they marry well. Their father—taciturn, affectionate, mocking, distant, clever but not wise—is a ghost in the machine, his life the only thing blocking their fall from respectable comfort to quiet desperation. They must find love because Mr. Bennet will die. Only romance can vanquish the ghost.

Nerd Note: Confidential to the *Pride and Prejudice* superfan who always took the Bennets' inheritance problem as a given: as you know, the estate has been "entailed in default of heirs male," meaning it will pass to a male relative if Mr. Bennet fails to have a son. It's conceivable Austen is implying that Mr. Bennet set up this arrangement in exchange for cash when he was younger, figuring he'd one day have a son. This would explain Mr. Bennet's tension with his extended family as well as Mrs. Bennet's anger. Even if Mr. Bennet isn't responsible for the entail, if Austen understood enough about legal terminology to knowingly choose the phrase "entailed in default of heirs male" (as opposed to another phrase, "strictly settled") she might have been implying that Mr. Bennet was in fact able to contest this state of affairs and at least try to leave the estate to his daughters.

This threatening state of affairs might be Mr. Bennet's fault, either because he refuses to stand up to social and familial pressure to contest this legal arrangement or because he himself is responsible for the arrangement in the first place. In any case, Mr. Bennet is dismissive of his wife's fears to the point of cruelty, once even stating that he hopes she dies first. Whether he's legally inept or knowingly damning his daughters to destitution, Mr. Bennet certainly has a touch of the sadist about him.

But if he's bad now, Mr. Bennet's legacy will be even worse, and this grim future attends his girls from birth, a lurking presence, something in the air. What is that bump in the night, that quiet murmur coming from the library? It's Mr. Bennet, and when he dies, his past will ruin us all.

Mrs. Bennet Is the Haunted House Historian

But *is* the entailment all Mr. Bennet's fault—I mean, did Mr. Bennet take one look at his hot wife and gamble the estate, assuming they'd have a boy eventually? Or is this intergenerational sexism at play, a long-standing arrangement Mr. Bennet either refuses to stand up to or doesn't realize he can undo? We don't know. We won't know. Only Mrs. Bennet knows. She is the haunted house historian, the character who knows the backstory, the one who understands how we wound up in this mess. The more she sounds the alarm, the more Mr. Bennet teases her—is it any wonder she feels like she's going batty?

Mrs. Bennet is the haunted house historian and she is *pissed*. She has given her life, her body, her beauty to the project of having a boy. In so doing, she has also become an additional horror trope: the mother of monsters, spawning and neglecting creatures who will end up feeding off society if they can't form a parasitic bond with the first eligible man who comes their way.

And what would it mean to save them, to save herself? Trapped between impenetrable legality and a husband who will barely look at her, desperate for her girls to survive on the marriage market with only their beauty and charm to recommend them, Mrs. Bennet finds herself squirming under the weight of heteropatriarchal capitalism. Is it any wonder she's notoriously awkward? She's a monster and a mother in a maze and she doesn't know which way to turn.

Mr. Collins Is the Attack of the Monster Appendage

If the Bennet sisters are up against horrors of all kinds, from the prospect of economic and social ruin to the lure of seductive predators and the haunting injustices of the past, then Mr. Collins is a monstrous appendage, a talking head and grasping hand hoping to pick one of them off. First he goes for Jane (she is the prettiest one and must be punished), but he's easily redirected toward Lizzy, and only by risking her life and future can our heroine avoid his cloying grasp.

Charlotte Lucas Is Living Another Person's Nightmare

Lizzy's BFF, Charlotte Lucas, is focused on her own survival. Without good looks or great fortune, she's fighting for her life without a weapon, and has to game the system instead. Mr. Collins came to town for a wife and a wife he shall have, and it doesn't take much to win him over. Soon Charlotte has a proposal, a comfortable home, and the promise of moving into Longbourn later.

But Mr. Collins's company is so grating, Charlotte will need to set up her living quarters to avoid running into him. By trying to avoid the fate she expected, that of dying an old maid, Charlotte has yoked herself to a ridiculous, obsequious creature who can never understand her, truly love her, or be her equal. She'll inherit her best friend's house, sure, but she's also living her best friend's worst nightmare.

Jane Bennet Dwells in the Uncanny Valley

Jane Bennet is so lovely, so demure, so poised that the love of her life is easily convinced that she isn't what she seems and doesn't really care for him at all. She seems too good to be true, and her close-but-imperfect resemblance to a real girl (like Lizzy, who manages to keep it remarkably real considering the amount of pressure she's under) arouses suspicion if not outright disgust in a reader—or a suitor, or a suitor's nosy friend—who expects a little humanity. She's too pretty, too calm, too generous. She sees the best in everyone, always speaks with kindness, and means what she says. To survive in Regency England, women must be perfect. Just don't be *too* perfect, or you'll end up in the uncanny valley: not quite a hot girl, not quite an automaton, not quite a corpse.

Mary, Kitty, and Lydia Bennet Are the Weird Sisters

Given how badly Mr. and Mrs. Bennet wanted to have a son, it's no surprise that daughters three through five were disappointments, and largely neglected. Taken as a trio, Mary, Kitty, and Lydia are the Weird Sisters of the story. They lurk in the background, at least for a while, but they are cooking up some disruptive magic that will send others' expectations into a tailspin. There's Mary, the crone, a nerdy autodidact with poor self-awareness. And then of course there's Lydia, the maiden, a budding, naïve seductress whose sexual appeal and power will throw a wrench in her family's plans. Once we have a maiden and a crone, all we need to complete the archetype is a blustering, anxious, doting mother. Oh, what's that, Kitty? We forgot you were there.

Wickham Is the Bad Guy Who Wins

George Wickham is a serial predator who preys on fifteen-year-old girls. He's a seductive monster, a child eater, a vampire looking to extract sex and wealth from his victims. And while he fails in his plot to hold Darcy's sister for ransom, he ultimately gets his way, sleeping with Lydia out of wedlock and convincing her that his affection is genuine. When Lydia refuses to leave Wickham's side—and who could blame her, given the life that awaits her as a "fallen woman"—Darcy pays Wickham to make the marriage official. In so doing, he may restore the Bennet family to their social graces and make his own intended marriage less of a blow to his brand. But he also lets the bad guy win.

Lydia Is the Bad Seed

What happens if from the moment a young girl is born, you teach her that her birth has doomed the whole family? As the last daughter, Lydia is the bad seed, the one who promises to destroy the family by the very nature of her birth. If she had been a boy, she could have saved them all, but because she is who she is, darkness promises to triumph. Neglected by her father, spoiled by her mother, and deemed useless from the start, Lydia, much like Frankenstein's creature, must rely on overheard chatter to figure out how to be and what to do. (Is it any wonder she's obsessed with gossip?) And the message is simple: only through marriage can you save yourself and the people who are supposed to love and care for you.

But the systems in place for finding a husband won't work for Lydia. She's the youngest, and not the prettiest, and she has no fortune to her name. Luckily she is also the tallest and has "high animal spirits"—she can embrace her monstrosity and take matters into her own hands. Leveraging her youth and her raw sexuality, she becomes an enfant terrible, a monstrous child, a dangerous flirt who will stop at nothing until she has imperiled herself and her family. But this peril is also her ticket out, a workaround, a blistering shortcut. By absconding with a monster, she makes herself a damsel in distress, and our "hero" has to rescue her. He does this by chaining her to her predator, sure, but we don't know what happens after our beauty and her beast tie the knot.

Perhaps Lydia is buried alive, forever yoked to a man who does not and cannot love her. Perhaps she reminds us not to go in the woods, not to circumvent the places and spaces and roles we are expected to fill, because there are always creatures lurking in the shadows. Or maybe Lydia is a body of bodies, the conglomeration of all her family's hopes, dreams, failures, and sins, a creature that cannot be contained by society and that will do anything in its power to break loose. Austen's narrator tells us she lives an "unsettled life," meaning she and Wickham move here and there, sometimes together, and sometimes apart, but I'm not sure I buy it. Maybe Lydia stays with Wickham, and maybe she takes off again.

Elizabeth Bennet Is the Final Girl

The marriage market is a dangerous game. Lizzy wins, and the rest of you can pack up and go home. If you have a home to go to, that is.

Put another way, Lizzy is the final girl, the girl in a horror movie who—generally because of her moral righteousness—is allowed to live to the end, and even defeat the killer.

Remember the first time Lizzy spots Darcy? They're at a ball where there aren't enough men to keep the ladies busy on the dance floor. (England is at war with France and lots of men have gone off to kill or die.) Darcy isn't dancing, and Lizzy isn't dancing, but instead of asking Lizzy to dance, Darcy ignores and insults her. (Remember, he tells Bingley that it would be a "punishment" to dance with any of the available partners and says that Lizzy is "tolerable; but not handsome enough to tempt *me*.")

This might seem like the end of their story, but Austen knows something we don't know yet, something Lizzy will learn that will let her escape with her life and something the book will teach us and reteach us for generations. It's no big deal if your soulmate overlooks you the first time he meets you. Disinterest and casual cruelty make a guy more interesting; the chase will be such fun!

In other words, if you want to make it out alive, you'd better learn to love a monster.

What Might Have Happened to Lydia If She'd Escaped?

If Lydia had left Wickham after running away with him, she could have expected a life of marginalization. If she had already become pregnant, her child would be born a hideous progeny unfit for polite society (for our horror tropes purposes: Frankenstein's monster). We can get a glimpse into the possible futures open to Lydia by looking at some of Austen's other characters who succumb to rakes.

- In *Sense and Sensibility*, a character named Eliza is seduced by a rake, left pregnant, and banished from polite society.

- In *Mansfield Park*, a wealthy girl named Maria settles for a marriage of wealth and convenience, has a passionate affair with the man she wanted before her marriage took place, and is publicly shamed in the papers, divorced, and forced to go live with her aunt.

- In *Emma*, the heroine's bestie, Harriet Smith, was born out of wedlock and has been left in the care of a school. Nobody knows who her parents are.

PART TWO

Bad Dudes:
A LITERARY
HISTORY

5

Love

BITES

or, A Field Guide to
Literary Monsters

*I*n the last chapter we said that Wickham embodies the trope of the bad guy who wins. Let's dig into that a little more, because in fact Wickham is a very *particular* type of bad guy, one who was a significant figure in novels of this period. Wickham is a rake, and rakes align with an especially indelible (perhaps we could even say *unkillable*) horror trope: that of the monster.

Wickham is also a foil character for Mr. Darcy, showing him as the ultimate ideal man in contrast to Wickham's rakish tendencies. What that means, though, is that Darcy and Wickham need to have a lot in common, in order to throw their differences into relief. The perfect suitor is, necessarily, really close to being a bad guy. What if we understood Mr. Darcy not as the ideal man but as the hottest monster in all of literary history? After all, as this chapter will show, the line between hot guys and monsters was pretty thin in the early nineteenth century.

Hot Monsters 101: The Rake

In Chapter 3, we discussed how Jane Austen looked back to the more reality-based novels of the early eighteenth century through the fun house mirror of the sometimes-paranormal Gothic novels she devoured. One character type Austen grabbed from these earlier novels (which we see in the Gothic as well) was that of the rake. At best, a rake is a seductive gentleman with designs on your virtue, your money, or both; at worst, he's a rapist. Whether you follow him of your own volition or find yourself tricked or trapped, any indiscretion might lead to your social (and, as in the case of Samuel Richardson's *Clarissa*, literal) death. So watch out. Don't let him touch you. Don't let him ruin you.

Austen uses the figure of the rake in her novels all the time. They're monstrous creatures lurking at the margins of polite society, brushing up against your arm at a ball, offering a crooked smile over tea. In *Sense and Sensibility*, Jane Austen's novel of two sisters with opposing temperaments, John Willoughby is the rake. A dashing young man with a mysterious past, he makes quite the romantic entrance, rescuing the more sentimental sister, Marianne Dashwood, when she slips on the rainy ground and hurts her ankle. Over the course of their increasingly intimate acquaintance, Willoughby flirts with Marianne and even cuts off a lock of her hair, a sentimental gesture that quite literally entails taking (a piece of) her body for himself. Willoughby takes Marianne alone to the house that he tells her, or at least implies, will be theirs, and shows her all the rooms, and I mean *all* the rooms. Then he abandons her, leaving her faded, avoiding society, desperate to speak to him—and, though Austen never says this explicitly, probably pregnant. Her life is restored to her only through a self-inflicted illness that requires an apothecary—i.e., a person who might be able to assist with a miscarriage or induce an abortion. If this reading seems too speculative, we might note that Willoughby has already, by this time, abandoned another young girl, whom he has definitively gotten pregnant. In the end, Marianne isn't ruined, she just ends up marrying an older guy, but she comes pretty dang close.

The rake in *Pride and Prejudice* is Wickham, who tries to trap Darcy's little sister into marriage in order to access Darcy's fortune, and who eventually runs away with Lydia instead. He probably has no intention of marrying her, but he gets trapped into doing so—by Darcy.

Rakes are the original sexy vampires of British literature: they draw you in and then they suck the life out of you. Rakes exist in real life, and chances are you've kissed one at some point. And the stories we cozy up to are full of rakes. Barney Stinson from *How I Met Your Mother* is a rake. Chuck Bass from *Gossip Girl* is a rake. Anthony Bridgerton is a rake, and when he falls in love with Kate Sharma he slowly but surely becomes a reformed rake, another eighteenth-century trope. But none of these fictional rakes can hold a candle to the greatest rake of all time, the one and only Lord Byron.

Mad, Bad, and Dangerous to Know

At once a fuccboi poet and an early celebrity in the modern sense, George Gordon Byron, the sixth Baron Byron, had an outsize effect on his cultural landscape, and ours. Whether you're familiar with Byron's storied life or whether this hot goss is new to you, odds are good that you're familiar with the Byronic archetype, the moody, introspective antihero at the heart of so many of our cultural touchstones. Byron first developed and attached himself to this archetype in his early work *Childe Harold's Pilgrimage*, a very emo and obviously autobiographical poem about a moody young man's adventurous travels. Applying old-timey poetic effects to a loosely anonymized story of his own travels across the Mediterranean, Byron published the project in installments with the first parts appearing during his trip, and returned home to find himself a sex symbol and superstar. Everybody in England, it seemed, wanted a piece of Byron, and he had affairs with everyone from Mary Shelley's stepsister to the aristocrat and Gothic novelist Lady Caroline Lamb, who termed him "mad, bad, and dangerous to know." Byron married a mathematician; their daughter, Ada (now commonly known by her married name, Ada Lovelace), would create what many people refer to as the first computer algorithm, but Byron wasn't ultimately a part of Ada's life. His wife divorced him, in a flex that was incredibly rare for women in the nineteenth century. It probably helped her case that Byron was having affairs with a range of men (including much younger men) and women, most likely including his own half sister. (It is worth noting that Byron's wife, Anne Isabella Milbanke, had definitely read *Pride and Prejudice* in 1813, and had called it the "fashionable novel." Is it possible that, by the time she married the elusive literary celebrity who would break her heart, she had already fallen hook, line, and sinker for the Darcy myth?)

As his fame veered toward infamy, Byron took off, renting a villa on the shores of Lake Geneva. Among his party was emo try-hard

Meet a Darcy

NAME: Lord Byron

LOVE STORY: Early-nineteenth-century British celebrity culture

TURN-ONS: People. Just, like, all the people. And sex. And himself.

TURN-OFFS: Anybody expecting anything of him, ever.

If you're looking for a frolic with the most iconic, genius fuccboi poet of the nineteenth century, bad boy Byron might be your man! This sexy beast is a total lothario, so if you manage to get time alone with him, you'd better make it count. He's liable to drop you like a hot potato for the next exciting prospect, and you never know when he's going to up and leave the country, either in search of adventure or to get ahead of the rumor mill.

Fun fact about our funky friend with benefits: while Byron seems to have no moral code when it comes to the dating scene, he harbors deep revolutionary ideals, the kind of love of liberty that is liable to get a lover boy killed in the Greek War of Independence. So, if you want to make your move with Byron, you'd better get in there—there's no time like the present!

John William Polidori, a personal physician with literary ambitions who was being paid by a publisher back in London to keep a journal of his travels with the poet. (His aunt would later censor these journals, destroying evidence of their more scandalous content, and I will literally never forgive her.) The Shelley entourage showed up, including fellow fuccboi poet Percy Bysshe Shelley, literary genius and Virgo queen Mary Shelley, and Mary's stepsister Claire, who was pregnant with Byron's baby. The party explored the landscape, and the landscape of one another's minds (and maybe bodies?), under eerie orange-tinted skies and strange weather patterns, both caused by a far-off volcanic eruption. Then, one night, they sat down to write scary stories. Byron produced an odd little fragment, a fragment Polidori took and extended into a novella. The novella drags Byron, using him as the basis for its antagonist, a seductive, debauched aristocrat who'll win your heart and suck your blood. That's right: a nineteenth-century fuccboi poet was the template for our modern idea of the vampire.

The Vampyre

Is Polidori's *The Vampyre* a masterpiece of nineteenth-century fiction? No, it is not. It did sell like hotcakes in its day, probably because publishers attributed it to Byron "by accident," a convenient accident that dealt a killing blow to Polidori's already unsuccessful writing career, making him look like a plagiarist and a hack. But a work of art doesn't have to be good to be incredibly influential. By turning a major cultural icon into a literal monster and defining the vampire as a seductive, secretive aristocrat, Polidori blurred the line between monster and man, offering a new version of the rake to generations of unsuspecting, swooning tweens.

In the case of the Byronic vampire, the threat posed by the rake becomes just strange enough to be palatable. The threat of real, damaging, physical violence is transformed into symbolic violence—and symbolic violence can constitute a safe place in which to contemplate lust and desire, because it doesn't correlate with real fears. It's not like you want to have sex with the *real* Byron, who claimed custody of Mary Shelley's niece just because he could and then left her in a convent, where she died. You want to have sex with the *idea* of danger. For a more contemporary (and possibly more familiar) analogy, think of *Twilight*, a direct descendent of Polidori's story. It's not that Edward Cullen wants to force Bella into sexual acts—that would be criminal and cruel. That would trigger the reader's worst fears and darkest experiences. No, he just wants to eat her! It's all good.

The problem is that this still teaches young women that a man who restrains himself from hurting you when he wants to is a *good guy*, that someone can remain your soulmate even after they've admitted they sometimes want to devour and destroy you.

Notably, while Polidori's iconic take on the vampire would catapult Byron's problematic vibe into an undead eternity, Byron and Polidori weren't the only Romantic-era writers to play around with the idea of monstrous characters who seem kind of undead. For a particularly spicy example, take Samuel Taylor Coleridge's unfinished narrative poem "Christabel," written around the turn of the nineteenth century. With its singsong cadence and old-timey medieval setting, "Christabel" gave Coleridge the perfect opportunity to think through one of those great philosophical questions he was known for—in this case, what would happen if a lady found another lady moaning in the woods? This moaning mystery, Geraldine, tells the heroine of the poem, Christabel, that she has been left under the tree by warriors who kidnapped her. (Sexy villains love an improbable backstory.) Christabel takes Geraldine in, but as the two women head to bed together, it quickly becomes apparent that something supernatural is afoot and that Christabel is in grave danger.

Or consider John Keats's "Lamia," in which a young man dies after marrying a woman who turns out to be a monstrous serpent— and who vanishes once she gets called out. For Keats, whose ailing health and finances prevented him from marrying the woman he loved, the snake who ghosts you might have embodied not transgressive desire, but the pain of disappointed hopes.

In the Dark

Byron may have been, in many respects, a bad dude, but he was also someone passionately committed to living his truth at a time when intimacy between men was illegal in England. While Polidori's vampire devours women (including, ultimately, the main character's sister), the truly subversive force pulsating beneath the novella is the bond of secrecy between two men. Indeed, the fragment of Byron's writing on which Polidori based his story doesn't necessarily have anything to do with vampires, but it does include a scene in which one character convinces another not to tell anyone he died. This sleight of hand is the turning point in *The Vampyre*—the protagonist knows the secret of Lord Ruthven's monstrosity, a life-eating force underlying his suave demeanor, but has promised not to tell anyone the lord is undead and cannot, will not break his oath.

Vampire stories since Polidori's have played with the theme of subversive sexuality, and J. Sheridan Le Fanu's *Carmilla* is no exception. I don't want to spoil this lesser-known classic of the vampire genre for you; for our purposes, it's enough to mention that Le Fanu uses the idea of a vampiric young woman feeding on the object of her hunger and desire as a monstrous metaphor for those other, forbidden intimacies that might exist between women behind closed doors. Take, for example, this moment from *Carmilla*, told from the perspective of the unsuspecting heroine, Laura:

> Sometimes after an hour of apathy, my strange and beautiful companion would take my hand and hold it with a fond pressure, renewed again and again; blushing softly, gazing in my face with languid and burning

eyes, and breathing so fast that her dress rose and fell with tumultuous respiration. It was like the ardour of a lover; it embarrassed me; it was hateful and yet overpowering; and with gloating eyes she drew me to her, and her hot lips travelled along my cheek in kisses; and she would whisper, almost in sobs, "You are mine, you *shall* be mine, you and I are one for ever."

In *Carmilla*, as in *Pride and Prejudice*, love is dangerous, desire monstrous. Perhaps Carmilla is a rake like Wickham: good-looking, charming, and emotive, but really a liar and a threat through and through. (Perhaps Carmilla is also a bit like Darcy, a sexy aristocrat who shows up unexpectedly and who simultaneously repulses and attracts you.) Laura, like Lydia Bennet, is preyed on by a seductive creature with a dark secret. Both must fight to make it out alive, whether socially or literally. Wickham is a rake reinventing himself as a militia man, the specter of war providing cover for his past folly, squandered opportunities, and attempts at cruel predation. Carmilla is an undead monster eating a young girl, an aristocrat from the past who literally devours the future. The tales are from different historical moments (*Carmilla* was serialized in Ireland almost sixty years after *Pride and Prejudice*'s 1813 publication in London) and, like many monster narratives, they are both a bit moralistically wonky, simultaneously punishing transgressions and creating literary spaces in which the idea of those transgressions can be explored. And yet, Austen and Le Fanu offer some of the same warnings: guard your body, guard your heart, and don't fall prey to wicked desires.

Sexy Beasts

Falling prey to wicked desires is, after all, exactly how one ends up being ruined by a rake. But what Byron and Austen both acknowledged is that the rake is often the most titillating character in the

Meet a Darcy

NAME:	Lord Ruthven
LOVE STORY:	*The Vampyre*
TURN-ONS:	Devouring people, destroying people, secrecy
TURN-OFFS:	Broken promises

He might bite your girlfriend. He might devour your sister. But he's not as boring and basic as all that. No, Lord Ruthven lives for the drama, and what's more dramatic than dying in front of your buddy on vacation, making him promise not to tell anyone you died, and then showing up as a *literal undead monster* and getting engaged to his *sister*? Honestly, somebody call Bravo, because shit's about to go down.

The best part of that whole secrecy thing is that your pal gets to go cuckoo bananas while he watches you plot his sister's demise. He's powerless to stop you. Is that a tribute to your supernatural power, or just a thesis statement on the strength of a sexy secret? Lord Ruthven will never tell.

story, and that this archetype could be elevated from the role of antagonist to that of romantic antihero. While *Pride and Prejudice* may not be *inspired* by Byron per se, its brooding, aristocratic love interest and Byron's brooding, aristocratic self-invention are part and parcel of the same historical moment and catered to some of the same cultural appetites, appetites informed by tropes of eighteenth-century fiction. Jane Austen sold the rights to *Pride and Prejudice* to her publisher in 1812, the same year Byron published the first two cantos of *Childe Harold's Pilgrimage.* Although Byron made himself a cultural event and Austen published anonymously, both writers fed into and indeed helped start the craze for moody, aristocratic antiheroes. To truly understand Darcy, therefore, we need to situate him at the literary-historical moment when the figure of the rake crossed over into the figure of the hot monster.

What does it mean that the touchstone figure of contemporary romance came out of this context? For one, it means that, much as we might love Darcy, in order to get a full picture of his cultural impact we need to recognize that he bears the mark of both the rake and the seductive monster. While Wickham is the villain of *Pride and Prejudice,* Mr. Darcy—his foil character, childhood companion, and nemesis—is an ideal hero specifically because he's almost the same as Wickham, minus the danger. In some ways, Darcy is defined by the rake: first as a monster, through Wickham's narrative, and then as a "safe" choice for Lizzy, through his rejection of that narrative. In other words, Darcy is a romantic figure and a Gothic figure at the same time. Bolstered by privilege, shrouded in mystery, image conscious and implicated in a plot twist that can easily be read as a young girl's demise, Darcy serves as a reminder of the very un-romantic realities that can befall a woman who doesn't keep close watch over her desires. Indeed, if she isn't careful, they might swallow her whole.

Twelve Stories That Are Secretly About Having Sex with Byron

THE VAMPYRE: LITERALLY WHAT ELSE WAS IN THAT JOURNAL, I am so mad. Were Polidori and Byron having an affair? Did Byron steal a partner Polidori was interested in? All of this seems likely, and more! I would LIKE A WORD with Polidori's MATRON AUNT. I would also appreciate a TIME MACHINE.

THE LAST MAN: I'm cheating a little with this one, because Mary Shelley's dystopian plague novel was really an elegy for her lost friends and loved ones, and the most crush-worthy character in the book, Adrian, Earl of Windsor, is certainly inspired by Percy Bysshe Shelley. But Lord Raymond is based on Byron, and Lord Raymond can get it.

WUTHERING HEIGHTS: Heathcliff, it's me, it's Cathy, you're so mean and brooding, you're so mad and bad, you're so dangerous to know, and yet people think this is a love story, and fans travel to Haworth and throw themselves on the sofa where Emily Brontë died. Because Byron.

VARNEY THE VAMPIRE: This serialized vampire tale, sold in Victorian penny dreadfuls, racked up a word count to rival any bestselling YA series of the modern era.

CARMILLA: J. Sheridan Le Fanu's seductive vampire is a beautiful young woman who speaks to her victim so ardently, she is sometimes mistaken for a suitor in disguise. Is she Byron? Maybe not. Is she Byronic? Absolutely.

DRACULA: While Bram Stoker's vampire isn't particularly sexy, and is grounded in years of painstaking (get it? staking?)

research on Eastern European folklore, the novel is very much about forbidden desires, including polyamory and same-sex love.

THE PHANTOM OF THE OPERA: He's misunderstood, OK?

INTERVIEW WITH THE VAMPIRE: Lethal monsters so sexy you'd cast Tom Cruise, Antonio Banderas, and Brad Pitt to play them? You guys, Polidori would have loved Anne Rice so much.

THE SOOKIE STACKHOUSE NOVELS/*TRUE BLOOD*: In the first novel, Sookie has vampire sex with her vampire boyfriend while she's drinking his vampire blood for pragmatic vampire plot reasons. The whole thing gives her vampire visions and afterward she explains to the reader, "This was pretty exotic stuff for a telepathic barmaid from northern Louisiana." If there is a better sentence in any novel, I don't want to know.

THE VAMPIRE DIARIES: Sometimes a teenager falls in love with a 162-year-old vampire. All the time everybody wants to have sex with Byron.

THE TWILIGHT SERIES: He WANTS TO EAT YOU but he WON'T EAT YOU he's just going to WATCH YOU SLEEP in a SEXUAL WAY.

FIFTY SHADES OF GREY: It's Twilight fanfiction: the violent threat of the rake that had been made figurative now made literal again, but with consent. Anyway, it's Byron who ties the main character up, and Byron, via both his own fame and Polidori's creative interpretation, who has tied our fear of the rake to our love of monsters for generations.

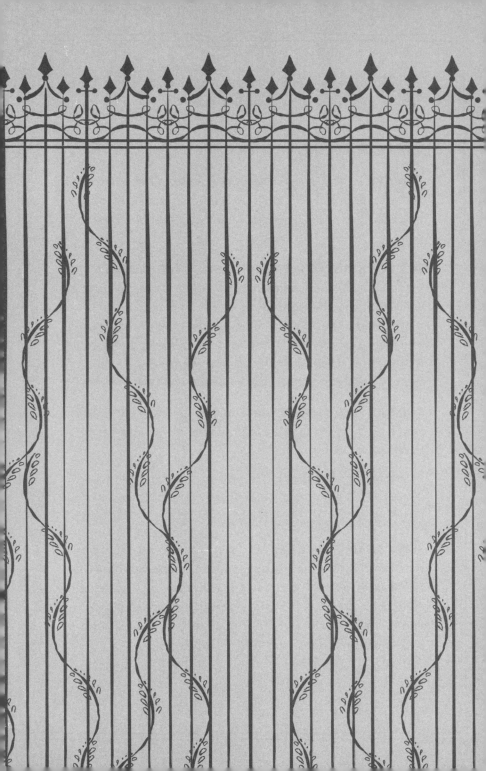

First

LOVES

or, The Monstrous Hunks
We Grew Up On

When Jane Austen wrote *Pride and Prejudice*, she drew on the Gothic novels she had read to produce a work that is both a love story and a scary story. Because Austen in general and *Pride and Prejudice* in particular have had an outsize cultural influence, this means that, inspired by Austen, we have gotten horror mixed up with our romance for generations. Recovering our understanding of the darkness in the love stories we hear and tell and share can help us navigate our lives and worlds in safer and more self-actualizing ways. When we realize that certain traits we've been taught make a potential partner appealing, like mystery or difficulty, also have the potential to lead us to the monster's lair, we can stop valuing the chase in and of itself and start evaluating the real person in front of us. Is the object of our affection just shy, or are they disrespectful? Are they awkward or actually mean?

This isn't to say we can't love enemies-to-lovers plots or see the good in people or even end up marrying someone who originally told their buddy we weren't handsome enough to tempt them. It just means that we can see the world—and see the project of love—without applying the Darcy filter, which teaches us to excuse bad behavior and seek out people (especially men) who treat us like crap. In other words, you can love Darcy all you want, but you're more likely to wind up living your *own* happily ever after if you stop viewing potential partners through the lens of the Darcy myth.

On the face of it, this sounds easy enough. After all, Jane Austen is dead! She's not about to show up at a house party and start selling us on the virtues of her "misunderstood" roommate. But even though our girl has given up the ghost and we have generations of feminist thought (including feminist thought inspired and bolstered by Jane Austen, even) to draw from as we make our way in the world, letting go of the Darcy myth can be hard to do. Why are we such suckers when it comes to Mr. Darcy? Because we've been taught, over and over, to love Darcy in all his forms. The training starts young, and the Darcy myth is so insidious in part because we're brought up on it.

Tale as Old as Time

I took my kids cabin camping with their cousins and ended up watching *Beauty and the Beast* in the forest.

Now first of all here is my thing with cabin camping. If there is no bathroom, it should count as camping. But somehow, as soon as there are walls, you don't get *camping cred*. Hot take: actually, I should get double cred, because it's harder for a two-year-old to wander out of a tent than it is for them to wander out of a cabin, which has a door. Additionally, although cabin plans were made (not by me), pillows were not packed, which means that I was personally moonlighting as a pillow.

Emotionally, Belle is moonlighting as a pillow, too. When we first meet our bookish brunette (and like many bookish brunettes of my microgeneration, I grew up *deeply* Belle-identified), she offers a lilting, heart-rending I-want song, delivered in part while walking through her quaint provincial town with her nose in a book (a trick I admired, but never was able to master). She tells us that she wants "adventure in the great wide somewhere" but what that ends up looking like for her is emotional labor with consolation prizes.

And, somehow, we're told that this is a happy ending.

Belle is a total lovable Lizzy—unusual, outdoorsy, curious. She's attached to her quirky inventor father and their unladylike draft horse. Belle rejects her self-possessed if hunky suitor Gaston (who, with his arrogance, flock of women hoping to marry him, and heart set on making Belle his bride, displays several traits that also dovetail with the Darcy archetype). When she discovers that her father has been imprisoned in an enchanted castle by a terrible beast who accuses him (incorrectly) of coming to gawk at him, she willingly offers to take her father's place. And when she does, there's that indelible moment. The beast tells her that, if she takes her father's place, she must promise to stay there forever. She asks him to come into the light, shuddering when she sees the full extent of his physical monstrosity and then bravely giving him her word anyway.

You guys. *You guys.* You. Guys.

I was six years old when this movie came out. Six years old. What did this teach me about love, and commitment, and marriage? Along with all the other little geriatric millennial horse girls, I was told that this is what gets you your happy ending. You find the monster. You take in the full extent of his cruelty, his difficulty, his horror. You give yourself to him (indeed, dragging Belle's father out of the castle before she can say goodbye, the Beast tells him "she's no longer your concern"). This is bravery. This is love. And then you wait, soaking up the emotions, the trauma, the hopes of his literal fucking cutlery. You run away and he chases you and he saves you and you save him and you dress his wounds. The petals fall and, even though they're a countdown toward your captor's permanent, beastly fate, each petal also takes you one step closer to the prince he always was. Patience is a virtue and your virtue is rewarded: with ballgowns, with books, and finally with his complete transformation.

Early in the Beast's metamorphosis, when love begins to change him from the inside out (A lie! People don't change unless they want to! You can't change him, only he can do that! Block his number! Sorry, I'm tired from cabin camping.), the Beast "gives" Belle his library, and this is exactly what I mean by consolation prizes. Books used to be her escape from provincial life—windows to the world, reminders of all the adventures she had planned—and now they're her succor and support in actual captivity. (This is how *The Bachelor* works too, by the way—you get married and then you make popcorn and watch a bunch of hardbodies compete for the captivity you've already achieved, and so you feel proud of yourself while you pity and mock them *while* you soak up the eye candy and indulge in the escapist fantasy of, like, vacationing in Norway with someone new.)

"It's yours"—what the fuck does that mean? Sure, it's a gift of books, but they're still contained in a room in his house, where Belle is a prisoner. And books are portals, windows, magic mirrors that reveal the freedom Belle is being denied.

Then Belle and the Beast flirt in the snow and feed birds and shit. Meditating on her developing crush on her captor, our beauty sings "strange . . . and a bit alarming . . ." Um, yes, it is fully alarming. You are his literal prisoner and you aren't allowed to see your family. Get out now, girl.

But we love the Beast, right? I fucking love the Beast. That he is somehow hotter as the Beast than as the prince he turns into is very, very telling. When the narrator poses that question at the beginning of the movie—"for who could ever learn to love a beast"—it's a challenge to the reader, er, I mean viewer. It's a preview to the movie and its message. You, little girl, must learn to love a beast, because that is your only way out, your only way up. Life is a trap and that's how you escape. Life is a love story and that's how you fall. And when Belle spits in her erstwhile suitor's face—"He's no monster, Gaston, *you* are"—she tells us a half-truth. Because Gaston and the Beast are two sides of the same coin. Both threaten to lock up Belle's father (the Beast in his castle, Gaston in an asylum) if she won't give herself to them forever. The only reason the Beast ends up a prince and Gaston ends up unalive is because the latter has been left to his own devices, while the former has been offered the life-changing magic of tidying up.

Now, *Beauty and the Beast* is based on a French fairy tale that predates Jane Austen, and nobody's saying that Jane Austen conjured the Darcy myth from thin air. But Austen captured our desire to fix a monster—to make softening up a bad boy our adventure in the great wide somewhere of his hot bod and enchanted castle, or whatever—in the hyperintellectualized bell jar of the Lizzy-Darcy paradigm. And *Pride and Prejudice* is definitely shimmering beneath the Disney version of *Beauty and the Beast*. We've already been over some of the similarities between Belle and Lizzy: beautiful, quirky ingenues treasured by their smart but somewhat peculiar fathers, dodging unwanted suitors despite the demands of their local marriage markets, and forging emotional and intellectual connections with soulmates they'd at first refused and despised. Both Belle and Lizzy realize they love their Prince Charmings (although Belle has told us earlier, in that same song, that the Beast is "no Prince Charming") after they fear it may be too late—Lizzy after she's rejected Darcy's proposal, and Belle after Gaston has stabbed the Beast in the back. Both heroines are rewarded with true love and glamorous digs after they put in the work—you know, complete self-sacrifice, patience, fixing a problematic man with their love and beauty, etcetera.

Here's my big issue with the ending of *Beauty and the Beast*, though. It's not totally clear that Belle ever *wanted* a prince and a castle. I thought she wanted adventures out in the world!

But this is precisely where things get Gothic as hell. In her initial I-want song, right before the bookseller gives Belle her favorite book to keep (a move that will be mirrored, later, by the Beast's gift to her, in captivity, of his library), she describes the book's story to him: "far-off places, daring swordfights, magic spells, a prince in disguise."

That's right, friends. Much like Jane Austen, Belle reads fantastical novels, and much like Austen's characters, she reads her own life into them. And she will be trained by them—trained to uncover the prince in disguise, to discover that it's him in chapter three, to make his transformation into the prince he always was her grandest adventure.

Our Favorite Crime

While *Beauty and the Beast* may be a touchstone text of my weird little heart, this type of romantic education isn't limited to those of us old enough to have had a Lisa Frank Trapper Keeper (bring them

Meet a Darcy

NAME: The Beast

LOVE STORY: Disney's *Beauty and the Beast*

TURN-ONS: Captivity, literal physical beauty, someone falling in love with him despite his apparent monstrosity

TURN-OFFS: Hospitality, being nice when he has nothing to gain

Who could ever learn to love a beast? Maybe *you* could—that is, if you like musty, enchanted castles, animate objects, ballroom dancing, and all things beastly. A fun fact about the Beast is that he's got a great library, and another fun fact is that his crush on you has extremely high stakes for a whole lot of people.

But if you like 'em rugged, and even somewhat cruel, then the Beast's intense lumberjack appeal might be for you. Just make sure you reject the toxic human man who is after you for your beauty. What is this, amateur hour? You'd rather melt the heart and hairy façade of a prince in disguise who is into you because you are literally any woman at all.

back, please, but for grown-ups). In January 2021, Olivia Rodrigo, teenage star of the Disney+ show *High School Musical: The Musical: The Series*, which is apparently the actual name of an actual show and not a joke told by the ghost of an absurdist playwright, released "Drivers License" and the internet exploded. In the song, Rodrigo's lilting vocals capture the aftermath of a devastating breakup, the singer driving past her former lover's street. In response to the song, emotions swelled, reactions raged, and rumors swirled on an outsize scale, with the impact of the song reaching far beyond the audience of Rodrigo's show. General consensus quickly settled on Rodrigo's costar Joshua Bassett as the heartbreaker, although the two had never publicly dated, possibly because Rodrigo was underage at the time of their alleged relationship. The "blonde girl" mentioned in the song, Rodrigo's growing legion of fans decided, must be fellow Disney star Sabrina Carpenter.

On TikTok, listeners sang along, cried, and analyzed the song in their cars, sometimes with a canny self-awareness about the bop's ability to transcend demographic barriers. For example, in a video posted by creator @rod, a thirty-year-old man offers a close-up of his emotional face as he sings along to Rodrigo's lyrics, the captions shifting along with his emotions from "checking out the new song all the kids are raving about" to "listening to a girl talk about getting her drivers license for the 80th time." The video has more than 120 thousand likes.

Why could so many people relate to a love triangle among Disney stars? Because so many of us have had an experience like the one portrayed in Rodrigo's song. This is, in part, because we have all been fed the same fairy tales. The reaction to "Drivers License" shows us that, no matter how aware and self-aware we get, the Darcy virus mutates, finding new ways to get into our bones.

Following her hit single, in late May 2021 Rodrigo released her debut album, *Sour*. An extended elegy for a failed relationship, the album offers a coherent narrative with only a couple thematic departures. Whether we think the album is about Bassett or not, and whether we think Bassett is a Darcy or not, there's no question that the narrative of the album embodies the Darcy myth.

The songs on *Sour* (mostly) tell us a love story, sure, but also a story about insecurity ("I'm not cool and I'm not smart / and I can't even parallel park") and betrayal ("remember I brought her up / and you told me I was paranoid") and disempowerment ("Like, am I pretty? Am I fun, boy? / I hate that I give you power over that kind of stuff"). Despite Rodrigo's youth, the story here is not one of innocence, or even of innocence lost, but rather of experience and understanding. And indeed, when we're brought up on the Darcy myth, we're taught that it's our job to see the prince in the beast, just as in "Drivers License," when Rodrigo sings, "all my friends are tired / of hearing how I much I miss you, but / I kinda feel sorry for them / 'cause they'll never know you the way that I do," and in "Good 4 U," when she asks, "remember when you swore to God I was the only / person who ever got you?" Despite the betrayal that pervaded the relationship and the unstable nature of their connection, Rodrigo sings that "I still fuckin' love you" and confesses, in a song aptly titled "Favorite Crime" (possibly alluding to her former underage status), "you know that I'd do it all again."

Put another way, Rodrigo, just like Belle, asks the beloved to "come into the light." And even though she shudders at what she sees, she still gives him her word.

The Punchline Goes

Let's talk about the Darcy myth (Taylor's version). In 2012, two years after a whirlwind romance with actor Jake Gyllenhaal, Taylor Swift released *Red*. The album includes what is widely regarded by fans and critics alike as her best song: "All Too Well," a meditation on a failed relationship that listeners might recognize all too well themselves—because it is a textbook Darcy myth.

'90s Movies that Taught Us to Love Darcy

The Lizzy-Darcy love story builds on a long history of bad ideas about love. And where better to look for bad ideas about love (and denim) than in one of my favorite literary movements of all time: movies from the '90s?

10 THINGS I HATE ABOUT YOU: In this high school retelling of Shakespeare's *The Taming of the Shrew*, Patrick is literally being paid to gaslight Kat and break her heart, yet she can't help seeing the good in him (and, to be fair, vice versa).

CRUEL INTENTIONS: Based on an eighteenth-century French novel, *Cruel Intentions* was the original *Gossip Girl*. Ryan Phillippe's character has to deflower Reese Witherspoon's character as part of a sex bet, but they fall in real love.

GOOD WILL HUNTING: This movie taught middle school girls everywhere to love math and also that men who love you might be mean to you—but that's just a result of childhood trauma that is not their fault.

CAN'T HARDLY WAIT: Has your childhood bestie become a player, or is he secretly still the sweet kid you used to know? You should probably get locked in a bathroom together and figure it out.

SHE'S ALL THAT: That popular guy played by Freddie Prinze Jr. may be dating you as part of a bet, but you can fix him! Getting contact lenses will help.

In "All Too Well," the poetess simultaneously mourns a lost love and stands up to the implied former lover, who might very well be trying to gaslight her into thinking their fling wasn't the great love of a lifetime. "Wind in my hair, I was there / I remember it, all too well," Swift sings, and we realize that we remember it too, because the experience of thinking somebody difficult or brooding or tall-dark-and-handsome but nine years older is really your Darcy in disguise is so culturally ingrained in us, it has reached the status of a near-universal experience. Even when the beast steps into the light, as it were, it's hard to believe the relationship wasn't what you thought. "Maybe this thing was a masterpiece 'til you tore it all up," Swift sings, and we believe her.

That's the thing about the Darcy myth, and about how it reproduces itself. "All Too Well" is a warning, but when you listen it feels like a fantasy. The scorned narrator of the tale is "the one real thing" the beloved has "ever known"; he can't get rid of her scarf because "it reminds you of innocence, / and it smells like me." He remembers too, and in this truth lies something foundational, something worthy of sacrifice (even if that sacrifice is your "old self"). Swift's textbook Darcy myth is also a storybook, one with a moral that might not be as clear as it seems.

In November 2021, Swift released a rerecorded version of *Red* in order to claim ownership of her work, her former label having sold their rights to someone she didn't want profiting off her recordings. The reclaimed version concludes with a ten-minute version of "All Too Well," a version Swift claimed was based on her original take on the song and one that made a tremendous cultural impact, quickly becoming the longest song ever to reach number one on the *Billboard* Hot 100. I am a happily married mother of two in my late thirties and I personally listened to the song on repeat with tears in my eyes while I baked a vegan pumpkin pie that was honestly just OK. Why did I sink into a delicious melancholy about Jake Gyllenhaal? Because I grew up on *Beauty and the Beast*, suckers!

Isn't that what the Darcy myth teaches us—that we should sacrifice ourselves to try to turn the beast into a prince? This is the story we're told and the story we tell. The short film Swift wrote and directed to accompany the ten-minute version of the song opens with a moment of pillow talk between "Her" (played by Sadie Sink) and "Him" (played by Dylan O'Brian): "Are you for real?" the young woman asks.

"What do you mean?" her lover replies.

"I don't know, I just feel like maybe I made you up."

There's something so canny about the wording of that question. "Are you for real?": are you telling me the truth about who you are, about how you feel, about what this is? Are you telling the truth or are you lying? And honestly, within the structures of the Darcy myth, what would lying look like? The beast doesn't lie about his monstrosity; he trusts that you've read enough books to recognize him as a prince in disguise.

But isn't "I feel like maybe I made you up" also an artist's statement? At the end of the film, "thirteen years gone" since her fabled love affair, our protagonist stands in front of a crowd, reading from *All Too Well*, a book with fabulous cover design. Sadie Sink is now Taylor fucking Swift—Taylor Swift with red hair reading from her book to a riveted crowd, no less. Taylor Swift recording a ten-minute version of a nine-year-old breakup song and topping the charts. "All Too Well" drags the former lover, sure, but at the end of the film he's in the crowd of admirers, too, just outside the glass, her scarf and scent around his neck. Turn your pain into art, "All Too Well" teaches us, and you win. You invent him. You get to keep him. You were there, you remember, and you can spin the yarn. You can re-record the song. You can tell the story for as long as you want.

In other words, by loving Darcy you reinvent yourself. Maybe you were an ingenue, just a girl in the world, but now you're an authoress, a songwriter, a poetess. By turning the pain of a failed relationship into the fruit of an extremely lucrative musical career—

one in which your art of persuasion is so powerful, you can ask your legion of fans to listen to a new version of a beloved album instead of the original, and they will oblige—Swift gives double cover to the Darcy myth. Maybe you can turn the beast into a prince, but if you can't, at least you can write a song about it. Even if he leaves you, by knowing him intimately you've captured him, and this intimacy, this knowledge, makes you an artist. For what is an artist if not a kind of beast slayer, someone who, like Ann Radcliffe in her Gothic novels, looks at the fear young women experience and elevates it to art? The Gothic is as cozy as a red scarf symbolizing the virginity you gave to the bad boy who will never be the same.

At one moment in her unfinished Gothic novel, the one she was writing at the time of her death shortly after giving birth to her second daughter (who would grow up to be Mary Shelley), Mary Wollstonecraft has her protagonist write directly to a daughter she fears she'll never see again. Offering this daughter a parting life lesson, Wollstonecraft writes: "I would then, with fond anxiety, lead you very early in life to form your grand principle of action, to save you from the vain regret of having, through irresolution, let the spring-tide of existence pass away, unimproved, unenjoyed.—Gain experience—ah! gain it—while experience is worth having, and acquire sufficient fortitude to pursue your own happiness; it includes your utility, by a direct path." The older man who doesn't show up at your birthday party may turn out to be your Prince Charming, but even if he doesn't, he's another Pokémon in your deck, another cute monster you've captured. And your ability to know him even in the face of his monstrosity, to give in to the power of experience, has all been to your gain.

And this is what I mean when I say the Darcy myth is insidious and constantly evolving. It takes as its touchstone Regency it girl Lizzy—who, with her muddy petticoats and sense of humor is, crucially, *not like other girls*—and hinges on Lizzy's ability to bring out a seemingly monstrous but actually idealized patriarch's softer side.

This sinister twist on girl power—the power specifically to mollify a man—means that the Darcy myth is programmed to adapt to our ever-evolving feminism and work around our self-awareness. That means there will always be a Darcy myth to grow up on for whoever is doing the growing up at any given moment.

When I was a kid in the nineties, Belle was there to reflect my bookishness and ambition and allergy to boys who cared about being cool, and then to teach me, by example, how to love a beast. For my students who have been Swifties since adolescence, "All Too Well" has recognized their emotional intelligence and self-awareness and depth of feeling, and asserted that the boy who fucked them up emotionally has only made them more interesting. But if the beast will give you a library, you're more likely to go in his castle, and if your tryst with an older man may help you become a successful artist, you're more likely to get in the car. "I see you, girl," the Darcy myth seems to say. "I see your easy playfulness or your charming bookishness or your undeniable connection with an older man that is no doubt the result of your personal maturity. I see you, and I've got you." But the Darcy myth has not got you. The Darcy myth has only one boss, and that's the patriarchy. And the Darcy myth has tried to teach you, from your earliest years, how to join the fold.

Quiz: Are YOU chasing a Darcy?

Read the following statements and give yourself a point for each one that applies to your current romantic interest. Tally them up at the end to find your result!

1. He teases you, but that's how you know he likes you.

2. Moments with him are magical, but he sometimes ghosts, or fades out, or is hard to reach or nail down plans with.

3. He seems embarrassed that he likes you or won't introduce you to his friends.

4. Your friends just don't understand your special connection.

5. Sure, he has a little bit of a bad reputation, but those folks are just jealous.

6. There are some red flags, but people are a work in progress, and you can fix him.

RESULTS

0-2 POINTS: He's not a Darcy, but he might be a little flaky.

2-4 POINTS: It might make sense to check in with this guy and make sure you're on the same page.

4-6 POINTS: Yep, he's a total Darcy. You should probably dump him and write a breakup song about it. Act fast, before he dumps you first!

7

Rakes

GONNA RAKE

or, Why We Can't Quit Bad Boys

*A*s we've discussed, eighteenth-century fiction is full of rakes, seductive men who will leave a woman ruined rather than respectably married. Some of these stock characters are simply serial predators, while others take the form of the reformed rake—the bad boy you can fix if you put in enough work. All of them bear some relation to literary monsters—and to Mr. Darcy, the *ultimate* fixer-upper. But who are the rakes of our day and age, how do they encode the rakes of previous generations, and what lessons—nefarious or otherwise—might they teach us?

I asked my English professor pals to share their favorite rakes. One colleague mentioned Beauplaisir, the dirty scoundrel of a love interest from Eliza Haywood's absolute banger of a novel, *Fantomina; or, Love in a Maze*. In *Fantomina*, the unnamed narrator dresses as a sex worker in order to engage the attentions of her crush without the restrictions of social formality. He rapes her. She then dons various identities in order to attract his attentions and have sex with him, which he sometimes believes is nonconsensual, and even puts on a mask to have *anonymous* sex with him. Shockingly, things don't go well for her, and her downfall is an object lesson in what it looks like to deal with a rake. You can try to mimic his predatory behaviors, or convince yourself casual is fine when that's not what your heart really desires. You can even fracture yourself into different personae in an effort to keep his attentions all to yourself. But no matter how hard you try to make him love you, eventually you'll just lose yourself. Because he's not complicated, he's just a rake. And rakes gonna rake.

Jane Austen was hyperaware of this trope and regularly played around with it. Her novels include classic rakes like *Sense and Sensibility*'s Willoughby, who seduces women and then abandons them, and *Pride and Prejudice*'s Wickham, who preys on young women in order to gain access to sex and money—and then decides the best way to cash out is to hold a teenage girl's honor hostage. There are more complicated takes on the rake figure in Austen's fiction, as well. For example, there are these sexy siblings in *Mansfield Park* that I'm low-key obsessed with. The brother, Henry, loves to flirt with women and play them off each other for fun. He's bored out in the country and decides to try and make uptight type-A super-Virgo heroine Fanny fall in love with him. In an extremely '90s-teen-movie move, Henry ends up falling in love with Fanny in the process. And then Austen does something fascinating: she gives Henry the total Darcy treatment. Being in love with a humble little creature like Fanny truly makes him a better man (or so it seems). He uses his connections to help Fanny's beloved brother William achieve promotion in the navy, and visits Fanny at her family's chaotic and much lower-class home in Portsmouth without judgment or loss of interest. But no matter how hard Henry tries to be the guy for her, Fanny keeps on rejecting him.

Scorned by the girl for whom he'd endeavored to change, Henry reverts from prince back to beast. He heads to the city and finds Fanny's cousin, a former object of his provocative attentions who has since settled for a marriage of fortune and convenience. Henry seduces Fanny's cousin and abandons her; the affair is written up in the papers, the woman's life is ruined, and Henry cements his reputation as a rake. (Oh, and Fanny gets to feel smug about refusing him and marries her almost equally uptight cousin. Go Fanny!)

What would have happened to Darcy if, despite his attempts to deserve Lizzy's love, she had been unable to overcome her initial hurt or squeamishness? If she had said, "thanks so much for paying your nemesis to marry my little sister so that you could marry me without sacrificing your brand too much, and thank you for admitting you were wrong to your bro so he could marry my older sister even though earlier you'd advised against it, but even though you're rich and handsome and have endeavored to correct your poor behavior in pursuit of my love, I'm just not that into you"? When Darcy offers his hand to Lizzy a second time, my students are quick to praise him for his "this is how I feel but no pressure" approach. In that swoon-worthy moment after Lizzy thanks him for essentially saving Lydia's life (while dooming her forever, obviously), Darcy says: "You are too generous to trifle with me. If your feelings are still what they were last April, tell me so at once. *My* affections and wishes are unchanged, but one word from you will silence me on this subject for ever." Austen doesn't tell us exactly what Lizzy says in reply—allowing us, instead, to put ourselves in her shoes and imagine it—but, once assured of her love, Austen tells us that Darcy replies "as sensibly and as warmly as a man violently in love can be supposed to do."

Now, let me be clear. I am not saying I think Lizzy should have said no to Darcy, or that I don't love this moment, or that this moment doesn't make me love Darcy. So before we proceed, maybe we should indulge in a collective swoon.

Swoon

OK, now that that's out of the way, let's get down to brass tacks. At this point in the novel, Darcy has sacrificed both pride and money to make Jane happy and Lydia respectable. He tells Lizzy that, in doing so, "I thought only of *you*." If his love for Lizzy or the promise of Lizzy's love has inspired Darcy's "good" deeds (setting aside for a moment that I think his actions in regards to Lydia are debatable at best), is the implication that he would stay good if Lizzy rejected him? Or is Darcy one "no thanks" away from a rake origin story? Austen does tell us he's *violently* in love, after all.

Now, to be clear, I'm not saying Darcy has the same character flaws as Henry Crawford. While a scorned Henry falls back on the powers of seduction, it's possible that a wounded Darcy would simply retreat into his pompous introversion, the beast roaring in his castle, his pain easily mistaken for monstrosity. Or maybe, with her various takes on the rake figure, Austen leaves a trail of breadcrumbs, leading us to ask what a man is capable of. Darcy is good—as long as he gets what he wants. And Darcy always gets what he wants.

While not quite a reformed rake, Darcy is certainly in the general vicinity of that trope—a man you couldn't have imagined marrying but are marrying nonetheless. And while not a rake, Darcy is certainly rake-adjacent; he is essentially a rake whisperer, able to figure out Wickham's location, divine his intentions, and talk to him in the language he understands (money). It's notable that Lizzy can't tell at first which one of them is the bad dude. If we want to be really generous, we could even say that, in reforming himself to become an eligible husband for Lizzy, Darcy reforms the rake himself, paying Wickham to make Lydia a respectable woman. Gothic scholar Daniel Kasper has claimed that "there are no reformed rakes, just books that end"; perhaps, for Darcy and Wickham, reformation is a sort of barter system in which sex, love, marriage, money, and pride are all up for grabs, and in which part of the goal is to keep your head above water long enough that you're still looking good when "happily ever after" rolls around. And maybe novels are barter systems, too. Much like Darcy pays off the rake in *Pride and Prejudice*, the Darcy myth functions as a permission slip for rakes in general by promoting the ideas that love is more valuable if it's hard-earned and that investing time and energy in emotionally unavailable people is a worthy romantic pursuit. What does the desire to reform the rake—to accept poor treatment while working to earn love—tell us about how we are socialized and what we think we deserve?

I first encountered Gossip Girl on a Vermont dairy farm. I was spending the summer between college and graduate school working for an arts program at a boarding school, and had convinced my kindergarten bestie, Sierra, to join me when a staff position opened up last-minute. The kids attending the program were high-school age, and some of the girls were passing around books in the Gossip

Girl series by Cecily von Ziegesar. At some point Sierra read the first few pages of one of the books and moaned, "I want to confiscate these and give them J. D. Salinger!" (Obviously in the fullness of time we both realized that Salinger probably would have been worse.)

I never did get around to reading the books, but I fell hard for the show after graduate school. I don't know, maybe watching teenagers acting like adults was exactly what I needed as I tried to enter the marketplace of ideas, or whatever. I do distinctly remember a moment during the era of my binge-watch when I was discussing the series pilot with Stephanie Insley Hershinow, an expert in eighteenth-century British fiction. She said, "listen, I work on the eighteenth-century novel, I know the rapist is often the most interesting character in the narrative."

The 2007 *Gossip Girl* pilot is a master class in the rake archetype; the rake in question is depraved prep-school pretty boy Chuck Bass. When we first see Chuck, he's lounging on a sofa flanked by two beautiful women at a society party. The camera pans to him when he calls out to ask if his friend has "any interest in some fresh air," which his hand motion indicates is a euphemism for smoking pot. When one of the girls he's sitting with reports that it girl Serena has returned to town, he swirls his drink and says, "good, things were getting a little dull around here"; when she shows up at the party and things get socially intense, he smirks at the drama. With just a few seconds of screen time, the show presents Chuck as a classic rake: dissolute, self-indulgent, debauched, a pleasure-seeker after his own entertainment. Reflecting on the party on the bus to school the next morning, Chuck tells his friend Nate—who we will later learn had a secret affair with Serena without realizing Chuck was voyeuristically watching—that he wants to force himself on Serena because her "level of perfection . . . needs to be violated." Later in the episode, he lures a drunken Serena into the kitchen of a hotel his family owns, pays the kitchen staff to leave while she's eating, and then tries to rape her. She physically defends herself and flees.

As if we had any doubt as to the nature of Chuck's character, he offers us a rake manifesto while talking to Nate, who is feeling trapped in his life and relationship. The conversation plays out as follows:

> **NATE:** Do you ever feel like our whole lives have been planned out for us? That we're just gonna end up like our parents?
>
> **CHUCK:** Man, that's a dark thought.
>
> **NATE:** And aren't we entitled to choose, just to be happy?
>
> **CHUCK:** Look, easy, Socrates. What we're entitled to is a trust fund, maybe a house in the Hamptons, a prescription drug problem. But happiness does not seem to be on the menu. So smoke up and seal the deal with Blair, 'cause you're also entitled to tap that ass.

Later, at a party, after asking "who's the newbie?" and telling us (surprise, surprise) that he loves freshmen, Chuck assaults another main character, the ingenue Jenny. Luring Jenny away from the party by asking if they can "talk somewhere private" and promising that it's "cool" if she doesn't want to "do anything," Chuck pulls out the eighteenth-century-rake playbook, getting Jenny alone where she can be violated. The narrator asks if Chuck will "end up with another victim." When Jenny's brother and Serena rescue Jenny, punching, pushing, and yelling at Chuck, the rake calls after Serena, "Your life is over, slut! Don't forget, I know everything!" He's referring to Serena's affair with Nate, who is dating Serena's best friend, sure, but he's also proving himself to be a true rake in the eighteenth-century mold by threatening not only Serena's body but also her reputation.

Rudely, my students stay the same age even as I get older, and it has been a while since I had a classroom of Austen students who love Chuck Bass to the point of having cardboard cutouts of him in their childhood bedrooms. Nonetheless, the popularity of the *Gossip Girl* universe persists, and it should absolutely repulse and frighten us that, following this pilot, the show manages to make Chuck a sympathetic character and desirable love interest over the course of its ensuing six seasons. The man is literally a rapist, and yet the show has us—and the teens to whom the show is geared—cheering for his "great love" with Blair and entertained by his romantic dalliances with the other characters. What's worse is that the show never quite reforms him; he stays dangerous, but that danger just gets folded into his appeal, Byron-style.

This is so problematic, and the Darcy myth is to blame. Indeed, the Darcy myth sets up the expectation that someone who seems terrible at first blush may in fact be hiding a deeper and better person inside—especially if that terrible-seeming person is a hot, rich guy. As the show weaves its soapy, intricate storylines, we get two things that we need if we're going to learn to love the beast that is Chuck: a traumatic backstory, and a redemptive romance. Sure, there is more plot than you can shake a stick at, and sure, Chuck goes on to do plenty of damage. But ultimately the show asks us to forgive and forget that when we first met Chuck, he was adding to his list of victims. This act of forgetting trains us to be victims ourselves.

This training is very gendered. Consider the relationship between the characters Hannah and Adam, played by Lena Dunham and Adam Driver, respectively, in the 2012–2017 HBO show *Girls*. While over the course of the show's several seasons this dynamic takes a lot of twists and turns (including some points when Hannah is the one rejecting Adam), when the show opens we see a rakish dating dynamic in which Hannah is having casual sex with Adam and seems to have more invested in the relationship than he does.

Meet a Darcy

NAME:	Chuck Bass
LOVE STORY:	*Gossip Girl*
TURN-ONS:	Violated beauty, pursuing a great love with an intellectual equal, pride and corruption
TURN-OFFS:	Morality

Love a good rake? Then you might catch feelings for Charles Bartholomew Bass. He's a poor little rich kid turned consummate bad boy, complete with perfectly fitted suits and a heaping pile of daddy issues (and mommy issues to boot). Sure, he's been known to take advantage and rack up a list of victims, but you can fix him. After all, only *you* can be his *great love*.

Listen: some of us are horny for depravity. There's no shame in that, or maybe the shame is the point. Maybe it's not about shame at all, and you just love a guy in an ascot. Whatever your taste, it might be time to let Chuck Bass sweep you off your feet and throw his bad behavior in your face.

The healthier periods in Hannah and Adam's relationship also follow Adam behaving aggressively as part of a not-fully-consensual sexual encounter with another woman he's dating. Does the show ask us to accept and forgive Adam for his sins, or are we supposed to embrace him as a Byronic antihero? In either case, the heteronormative, whitewashed world of the series sets up Hannah as a writer who claims to be "the voice" (or at least "a voice") of a generation, and the show sets itself up this way too, as a voice of a generation or at least the voice of (its very limited definition of) that generation's "girls." But the experiences of millennial womanhood that Hannah/Dunham presents to the viewer don't model a particularly impressive amount of self-respect. Instead, they give us a girl's guide to loving a rake.

But the rake archetype also transcends any particular identity. While the rake is a trope commonly applied to men in heteronormative relationships, other relationship dynamics can still be influenced by these expectations. Women can certainly be rakes, both in popular culture and in real life. In *Sex and the City*, Samantha's erstwhile beau Richard is clearly a rake, but Samantha's casual attitude toward sex and voracious appetite for encounters with men might be said to give her a touch of rakishness as well. Shane McCutcheon, the lovable, lanky lothario from *The L-Word*, is first introduced to viewers as "Don Juan." When she sees her place on her friend's digital map of LA lesbian hookups, she quips, "Look at that, I'm the center of the universe." While characters like Shane and Samantha are presented as less predatory than Chuck Bass—maybe partly because it's seen as normal for men to be predatory—these characters' abilities to follow their sex drives through the world without looking back derives from the rake archetype and sometimes leads to hurt and harm.

The figure of the rake initially developed as a stark warning to women who might face physical harm and social death if they trusted the wrong man. Don't get into his carriage, eighteenth-century fiction taught girls and women, even if he tells you that he'll take you home. In a modern context, where the idea of consent outside of the social and financial bounds of marriage makes sense, the rake figure has become increasingly complex. If you get in the rake's carriage of your own accord, then is the rake really to blame if you harbored some unfounded ideas about where the carriage was headed?

In *Pride and Prejudice*, Austen shows that the rake and the gentleman are two sides of the same coin. Indeed, when Darcy pays Wickham to marry Lydia and then marries Lizzy, we see the rake and the gentleman collaborate to uphold patriarchal norms by redirecting female choice and policing female desire. The patriarchal structures being upheld are, in this case, the literal patriarchy—the societal control wielded by fathers. Darcy's father meant to provide for Darcy and Wickham, but Wickham squandered what he was given; now he is forgiven, financially if not emotionally, and order is restored. Lydia has been neglected; her father has not kept her protected. Now Darcy, as a patriarchal figure, must step into a father role by paying Lydia's dowry to Wickham once she rejects the notion that she can or should be rescued. Lydia is punished for diverging from social and sexual mores, and is made a wife. Lizzy's countercultural decision to reject a man of fortune is rectified, and she is made a wife, too. While Darcy and Wickham are the agents of change within the world of the novel, it's really the novel itself—and, by extension, Jane Austen—that is upholding the status quo. When we follow the novel's implicit directive to focus on Lizzy and Darcy's meeting of the minds, it's easy to see their partnership as subversively equal, consensual, and based on mutual love and respect. I don't want to take that fantasy away from you, but I also want to encourage you to see the ways in which Darcy, though not quite a rake himself, aids and abets the rake. Additionally, one of the commonly cited morals of the story—that Lizzy must overcome her prejudice to see that Darcy is not a beast but a prince in disguise—has been aiding and abetting rakes (both fictional and flesh-and-blood) for generations.

Because overcoming your initial impression of a potential partner to see how great they secretly are can also involve ignoring red flags and seeing what you want to see, instead of what's true. Even if the beast you're trying to turn into a prince isn't an outright predator, you might still get hurt. This is what can happen when you fall for a rake, or for someone who errs on the side of rakishness when it comes to sex and love. You decide the carriage is going where you need to go when sometimes the carriage is going nowhere, it's just a really sexy carriage. Even if you see the carriage for what it is, and are getting in of your own free will, you still might need to ask yourself: are you trying to get home, or are you just along for the ride?

Signs You Might Be
Trying to Reform a Rake

If you're wanting more of a romance plot than the object of your affection is willing to give but hope you can get them to come around, then you might be playing out a tale as old as time: that of the reformed rake.

You might be trying to reform a rake if:

- You're the kind of person who owns a label maker, but the object of your affection has convinced you that you don't believe in labels.

- You think your relationship is more passionate and meaningful than one that feels easier and more comfortable.

- You blame your lover's dark past for their inability to treat you kindly or commit to you.

- You've tried changing your identity or personality in some way in order to ensure that a crush will stick around.

- Even though things didn't go well with this person before, you're convinced that this time, it will be different (because they've changed or because you can fix them).

Careful! At the time, these may seem like signs that you've found your Prince Charming. After all, the Darcy myth has been incredibly aggressive in its messaging. But if these signs persist and you find yourself feeling tired, frustrated, or disrespected, chances are that's not a prince in disguise, it's just a beast.

8

Twisted

LOGIC

or, Why Darcy and Heathcliff Have More in Common Than You Think

$\mathcal{R}$emember, Darcy is good as long as he gets what he wants. And Darcy always gets what he wants. Sure, he might need to sacrifice his pride and lay down some cash in the process, but he has every privilege going for him, and things tend to go his way. Austen is crystal clear about Darcy's pedigree and power, and teaches the reader to love and trust her leading man.

But is Darcy really as trustworthy as Austen leads us to believe? Or is he just someone who is large and in charge? Darcy's wealth and privilege make his decision to change (and to change his mind) for Elizabeth more meaningful—he changes when he doesn't have to. But isn't this also kind of a scary idea—that someone chooses to be good, or to be better, out of the goodness of their heart or to win over their crush and not because they really need to examine their actions in order to be successful and sought-after?

If Darcy is a little bit of a Byronic hero, and a little bit of a rake, then he's a little bit of a monster, too. Maybe we just never get to see the full expression of that monstrosity because Darcy is lucky as hell: rich, privileged, and untouchable. What might Darcy look like if he had shittier luck? One answer might lie in Heathcliff, the monstrous main character of Emily Brontë's 1847 novel, *Wuthering Heights*. Despite his readily apparent danger and cruelty, readers and writers adapting *Wuthering Heights* to the screen sometimes confuse Heathcliff with a romantic hero based on his intense and intensely frustrated emotional and sexual bond with the novel's antiheroine, Catherine.

If *Pride and Prejudice* is a love story haunted by the Gothic, then *Wuthering Heights*, which is mystery girl Emily Brontë's only known surviving novel, is a Gothic novel haunted by the marriage plot. A twisted family saga told within nested frame narratives, *Wuthering Heights* shows us what happens when a Byronic figure *doesn't* get what he wants, and decides to burn it all down instead.

The novel concerns the relationships among the members of two families, the Earnshaws and the Lintons. Both families are landed gentry living on the Yorkshire moors, a spooky landscape that becomes a character in itself, full of misty atmosphere, damp graves, and vast, grassy expanses where a girl might easily take a wrong turn. The disruptive force of *Wuthering Heights* is its antihero, Heathcliff, an orphan of mysterious origin whom Mr. Earnshaw brings home and raises among his own children. In addition to having a lower social status than the Earnshaw children, Hindley and Catherine, Heathcliff is coded as physically darker and thus racially other. Hindley is jealous of Heathcliff and treats him cruelly; when Hindley inherits the property of Wuthering Heights, he degrades Heathcliff from favored foster son to the status of a servant.

While Heathcliff's relationship with Mr. Earnshaw's other child, Catherine, is more positive, it ultimately wrecks him. Heathcliff and Catherine are soulmates, but she cannot bring herself to marry him, explaining to a servant that it would "degrade" her to marry him despite the fact that "whatever our souls are made of, his and mine are the same." Catherine chooses to marry Edgar Linton, a young man from the neighboring household, instead. Degraded, shunned, and rejected by the woman who loves him, Heathcliff leaves, makes his fortune, returns, and ruins everybody and everything. Imagine if Darcy's sister had married Wickham and Wickham had somehow gained Pemberley and Lizzy had rejected Darcy and, in a rage, Darcy had vowed that everyone who had wronged him would end up dead or destitute or locked in the closet until they agreed to do his bidding. That's the vibe of *Wuthering Heights*. The horror runs rampant, too—Catherine becomes ill from the drama and dies in childbirth and Heathcliff digs up her grave and is haunted by her ghost. If folks read Heathcliff as a romantic hero, it's either because they're focusing more on the passionate impossibility of his union with Catherine than on his acts of cruelty and abuse, or because they haven't done the reading. *Or* because the Darcy myth has done them dirty to the point that they mix up monstrosity with romantic love, full stop, as long as there's also kissing.

Hottie Smackdown:
Darcy versus Heathcliff

DARCY

DIGS: Gets the family estate when his father dies

LOVE: Can marry the woman he wants once he ruins her sister's life so he doesn't seem socially inferior

MOTIVATION: Preserve the family's honor (which is also his personal honor)

HAUNTED BY: The time his sister almost had sex

HAS A WEIRD THING FOR: His crush's dark eyes

HEATHCLIFF

DIGS: Gets the family estate when he wins it back from his brother through gambling

LOVE: Can't marry the woman he wants and is made to feel socially inferior; ruins everybody's lives

MOTIVATION: Seek revenge (for being dishonored and kicked out of his family)

HAUNTED BY: His adopted sister's ghost

HAS A WEIRD THING FOR: His true love's dead body

Like *Pride and Prejudice*, *Wuthering Heights* erodes the boundary between romance and horror Gothic—though it winds up way more on the horror side. Scholar of Victorian fiction Claire Jarvis explains that, because of the structure of Heathcliff and Catherine's masochistic relationship, "it does not much matter, in the world of the novel, what happens next. . . . Instead, it's clear that while Catherine the Elder and Heathcliff expect and want consummation from the first moment of their sensual embrace, they also build the intensity of their relationship through a series of masochistically inflected, erotic scenes. The anticipatory logic is so strong that, even after death, the yearning that structured the relationship during life remains." In other words, Heathcliff and Cathy want each other, but the nature and power of that wanting combined with their shared inability to give themselves to the other person creates an emotional explosion that does a lot of damage. And when you curate sexual and romantic desire but delay gratification and satisfaction indefinitely, you end up fucking a ghost.

This intense wanting—the kind of wanting that becomes an end in itself, and then puts an end to hope—is not as far removed from the Darcy myth as it might at first appear. Bear with me here for a second. Heathcliff is also the object of adoration. He also ends up with his family's estate. If you just met him on the moors, how would you be able to tell that the passionate crinkle in the corner of his mouth, his emotionally unavailable affect, and his sexual intensity weren't signs that he was your Darcy? Byronic, monstrous, yet just close enough to a romantic hero to give readers tingles down their spines, Heathcliff shows us how close a figure like Darcy is to depravity and reminds us that someone who seems similar to Mr. Darcy is not always someone we want to get involved with.

At one point in *Wuthering Heights*'s dark unspooling, Heathcliff kidnaps the dead Catherine's daughter (also named Catherine, also possibly his own daughter) and holds her hostage until she agrees to marry his sickly son. The purpose of this cruelty is to gain control of both family homes, thus exacting his revenge on those who have wronged him. He's also exacting a wicked revenge against young Catherine's father, who married his love—young Catherine isn't sure she'll make it home to see her father before his death. Heathcliff's imposition of past trauma on the next generation, then, is somehow also an act of putting his own generation to bed in as painful a way as possible.

While the abuse and cruelty Heathcliff inflicts on young Catherine place the novel firmly in the Gothic horror boat, the terror our would-be heroine experiences is all the result of a marriage plot that went awry. If the elder Catherine had simply married Heathcliff, Brontë implies—if she hadn't worried that his social status would degrade her but had instead watched the beast step into the light, revealing his mysterious past and dark impulses, and nonetheless given him her word—then none of this would have happened. Heathcliff and Catherine would have had a home together, either at Wuthering Heights or elsewhere. The revenge they exacted on Hindley would be, simply, the revenge of living well. They would have stood in the face of Hindley's attempts to degrade Heathcliff, and enjoyed their meeting of the minds, and relished the passion between them, and loved each other bravely and well.

Of course, if you've read *Wuthering Heights*, this type of counter-narrative feels next to impossible, because these are destructive and dysfunctional people who exult in torturing each other to the point that one of them literally dies. Heathcliff and Catherine are doomed to live a horror novel because of their acute inability to relate in healthy ways—an inability that results in intergenerational trauma. That Heathcliff is still attracted and drawn to Cathy's dead body proves that it was never about the meeting of the minds (or souls or what have you) in the first place. What Heathcliff and Cathy both want, on some level, is to want, and to try to win.

Setting aside that Heathcliff and Catherine's explosively destructive relationship seems to be the only relationship they are capable of having, the idea that the book's rising action is inspired by Catherine's choice of another man over Heathcliff plays into the Darcy myth in dangerous ways. If all of Heathcliff's monstrosity was inspired by Catherine's rejection, does the logic of the novel imply that Catherine is the true monster of the tale? Because she married the wrong person, she directly doomed everyone. Because she chose someone less rough around the edges than the soulmate who was essentially raised as her brother, Catherine has damned both families to misery and ruin. If the ability to turn the beast into a prince is in your hands, then doesn't that imply that the continued existence of the beast is your fault? *Wuthering Heights* is haunted by the marriage plot that wasn't, and the cause of this haunting is Cathy. The reader first meets Catherine when she is already a ghost, and she's a ghost because she refused to tame the beast.

In the spirit of the Gothic and its strange relationship to past and future, Emily Brontë plays around with different timelines in *Wuthering Heights*. We hardly know anything about Mr. Lockwood, one of the frame narrators and a tenant of Heathcliff's who hears much of the backstory from a servant, but we do know that he is distinctly Darcy-coded. Introducing himself to the reader (even though he's pretty much just a plot device), Lockwood explains that "my dear mother used to say I should never have a comfortable home, and only last summer, I proved myself perfectly unworthy of one." Lockwood's great sin, he tells us, was essentially ghosting a girl he liked. He calls her a "most fascinating creature" as well as "a real goddess," high compliments that are nonetheless dehumanizing. While Lockwood never confessed his love with words (much like Jake Gyllenhaal, who "never called it what it was" in Taylor Swift's "All Too Well"), his adoration was obvious, and the woman in question began to return his affection and respond to his attentions. In response, for a reason he doesn't explain, Lockwood confesses with shame that he "shrunk icily into myself, like a snail" and "retired colder and farther" every time the girl looked at him.

Meet a Darcy

NAME:	Heathcliff
LOVE STORY:	*Wuthering Heights*
TURN-ONS:	Sadism, revenge, being another person's shadow self
TURN-OFFS:	Degradation, abandonment

Do you thrive on the knife's edge between passion and hatred? Do you have a thing for orphans of mysterious origin who were low-key raised as your sibling? Or maybe you simply have a possessive streak so strong you'd rather your ex dig up your grave than find happiness with someone else? If so, Heathcliff might be the ride and/or die for you.

Maybe your favorite color is morally gray. Maybe you're more intense than the circus. Maybe you have a high tolerance for predatory behavior. Maybe you were taught, from your earliest days, to confuse hate with love, or maybe the eerie landscape is getting to you, or maybe your choices were always limited and there was never a good option, just two options that were bad for wildly different reasons, and you somehow wound up with the worst of both worlds.

Or maybe timing is everything. Maybe you can love Heathcliff for who he is, and claim him as your soul to his face, and stand together braced against the storm. Maybe your love can turn his luck, and turn him into a prince instead of a beast.

In Brontë's twisted logic, Lockwood's punishment for ghosting is an actual encounter with Catherine's ghost, who makes his crush's feelings literal when she begs to be let in from the cold. (By the way, did you know that Kate Bush, who took up this line in her famous song "Wuthering Heights," has the same birthday as Emily Brontë? This is Leo culture.) What *Wuthering Heights* teaches us is that Darcys are everywhere. Sometimes they've vanquished their enemies to build a real-estate empire, and sometimes they rent. Reaching through the broken windowpane of Victorian realism (think Charles Dickens) and through the genre-defining marriage plots of Jane Austen and other writers, Cathy's ghost grabs the Gothic in her cold little hand and reminds us that moody men of means are not always *nice*. Love can save your life but love can be the death of you, too.

Perhaps the Gothic reminders in *Wuthering Heights* can function as a kind of antidote to the Darcy myth. In an ideal world, the Gothic reality that Darcy with shittier luck might in fact be a very scary dude should remind us to avoid cruel men in the first place. But in order for *Wuthering Heights* to work on us in this way, we have to make sure we remember that it's not, in any sense, a romance.

Much like Jane Austen, Emily Brontë is a famously elusive historical figure, one who was mythologized after her death (largely by her sister Charlotte) and whose true character and intentions remain a mystery. But, if I can take some liberties for a moment, it might be interesting to think about how Austen's Gothic-haunted romance and Brontë's romance-haunted Gothic relate to their personal interactions with men. Neither Jane Austen nor Emily Brontë ever married. At one point, Austen accepted a marriage proposal from her friends' brother, but she changed her mind the next day, probably because she didn't particularly fancy him and decided not to settle. Her heroine Lizzy would get to have her cake and eat it too, rejecting a suitor she didn't desire and then finding her ideal match.

On another note, several years ago, a man approached a famous Austen scholar and claimed, quite convincingly, to be descended from Cassandra Austen's illegitimate child. Human nature being what it is, it's not particularly unbelievable that Jane Austen's best friend and sister, the Jane to her Lizzy, might have slept with her fiancé before they were wed. This seems particularly likely given that Cassandra's fiancé needed to earn more money before they could marry and so left for the Caribbean, where he died of yellow fever. If Cassandra did have sex with her fiancé before he left on his journey (and really, the more you think about it, doesn't this seem likely?), then it's certainly possible she became pregnant. In fact, despite strict social mores against premarital sex, scholars examining church records of weddings and births estimate that pregnant brides were not uncommon in Regency England. And if Cassandra became pregnant, as Austen's novels teach us it's likely Cassandra had to hide her pregnancy and somehow hide the baby to avoid ruining her family's reputation. So Jane's intimate experiences with betrothal, love, and a lack of choice could certainly have haunted her portraits of the social world. If you're convinced that Harriet Smith's anonymous parentage or Willoughby's or Henry Crawford's exiled former lovers are simple plot devices, remember that Jane Austen herself might have had a niece or nephew much like those banished babies. (This might even explain why Cassandra burned many, but not all, of the letters between her and Jane before she died.) Austen's marriage plots are haunted by the Gothic in part because women's lives in Austen's time were haunted by the threat of physical harm, true loss, emotional discomfort, and the always-possible fall from grace.

The dark and twisted nature of *Wuthering Heights* might derive, at least in part, from the author's life, too. Emily Brontë's tale of a heroine trapped in an abusive relationship with a friend and romantic interest who was raised as her brother may draw some of its emotional intensity from Brontë's relationship with her own brother, Branwell, a beloved playmate of her youth who descended into addiction in adulthood and was lost to his sisters long before he was really gone. Whether a novel's Gothic elements draw from the pain, hurt, and constant threats of a woman's actual life, or whether they speak to the threats against women that exist on a larger scale in an unjust society, the intermingling of this darkness with romance necessitates our attention. Would folks still be talking about *Wuthering Heights* if the relationship between Heathcliff and Catherine were purely platonic, a messed-up family dynamic between adopted siblings who viewed one another as such and nothing more? I doubt it, because that wouldn't be *sexy*. And society has taught us that women's pain needs to titillate us in order to be worthy of our attention at all.

It's no wonder that *Wuthering Heights* is Bella's favorite book in *Twilight*. It's a field guide to self-destruction; it threatens you with what might happen if you don't make the monster your problem. But, as we'll see, *Twilight* isn't a story like *Wuthering Heights*. It's not a story where the world order burns down and the survivors are left to try and start something new. It's a story more like *Pride and Prejudice:* a marriage plot, where someone who might seem like a Heathcliff is actually a Darcy with a complex backstory, where a monster controls his desire to eat you and instead commits to loving you for an undead eternity. And when we look at how and why our monster narratives are also Darcy myths, we can begin to understand how profoundly they have messed up our ideas about love.

9

Monster

FUCCBOIS

or, What Sexy Vampires
Understand About
Jane Austen

*T*o love a rake is to experience shame and shamelessness at the same time. The shame comes in sacrificing honor, or "purity," or reputation, in putting someone else's predatory needs above your own. The shamelessness comes in owning that desire, standing before the rake in a mask as if to say you don't even care who you are anymore.

In an episode of the TV show *Community* titled "Origins of Vampire Mythology," Britta finds out that an ex is in town and immediately gives her phone to her friend Annie, asking to be put on communication "lockdown" so she won't call or text. The situation escalates, and she ends up on literal lockdown, imprisoned in Annie's bedroom. (Annie also changes Blade's contact info in Britta's phone to her own number—which is good, because Britta is resourceful, and finds a way to send "Blade" a series of increasingly intense texts.) When she initially asks Annie to keep an eye on her, Britta asks to be chained to the radiator like a werewolf—essentially saying that treating her like a monstrous beast is the only way to keep her from getting in touch with the guy.

So who is the beast that makes her so beastly?

Well, the dude's name is Blade, and he works at a carnival. When another character, Jeff, heads to the carnival where Blade works to figure out his secret to captivating women, Jeff's initial impression is pretty straightforward: "He's a dirtball." He concludes that Britta must hate herself, and that's why she's so into a clear no-goodnik. Donald Glover's character, Troy, agrees: "Britta likes guys who are mean to her. She doesn't like herself."

But what if it's not so simple?

The episode's title alludes to *Blade*, a movie based on a Marvel comic about a vampire hunter. But, intentionally or no, it also alludes to the true origin of the Western vampire archetype: Lord Byron. And the show's ultimate explanation of Blade's appeal might reveal something about Lord Byron, and the Byronic figure, as well.

At the end of the episode, Jeff arrives at the scene of the lockdown. He has camped out at Blade's carnival booth, spending cash, winning stuffed animals, and digging for his secret. And finally, all has been revealed.

In a bracing moment of monologue, Jeff explains Blade's sexy backstory:

"Ten years ago, before he even met [Britta], a loose bolt flew off a Ferris wheel and embedded in his skull, destroying the part of his brain that feels shame. He's basically irresistible to people for the same reason he can pretty much only work at a carnival. He has nothing to prove or disprove about himself or to himself. He has no shame." Blade is not a monstrous human, in the end, but something more like a scapegoat. He has played the role of monster for Britta simply by not caring how he appears to others. He's just a guy with a Frankenstein-esque bolt in his skull who doesn't recognize, or care to recognize, the dangerous dynamics in which he's participating. He inspires Britta to act shamelessly because he simply cannot relate.

Lord Byron probably didn't lack the ability to feel shame, at least in general. But when it came to women, he certainly acted without shame, and inspired the same in turn. He left a trail of abandoned lovers and daughters in his wake. While Byron was a brilliant celebrity poet and Blade is a dirtball who works at a carnival, they're mythological beasts of the same mode, and they draw people in via the same mechanism. You can't make them care, and—much like Britta desperately texting "Blade"—you can't help but try.

Maybe, as the *Community* characters theorized, you can't help trying to make a monster love you because you don't like yourself. I mean, that's possible—the minute Troy, posing as Blade, replies to one of Britta's texts in a loving and affirming way, she decides that Blade's a loser. She's in it for the pain. But maybe, just maybe, you can't help trying because you truly believe you can fix the object of your adoration—and you've encountered a *lot* of cultural narratives promising that you're right. You can make them care. You can make them love you. You can turn the beast into a prince, or reveal that they were always a prince in disguise. You can prove that you're Lizzy, and they're Darcy, and if people think they're a monster, that's just a prejudice. Maybe what you harbor isn't self-hatred but a different, twisted type of pride—an unfounded faith in your ability to discover and reveal the handsome truth about an elusive hottie. And maybe this pertains to the strange ability of sexy monsters to embody both our fears and our desires. You want them, and you want to change them. And yet, on some level, you're experiencing the thrilling fear that you can't.

Maybe you imbibed this pride, this fear, these desires from young adult literature. Maybe I am going to talk about Twilight.

I read the Twilight books in graduate school, when I was supposed to be studying for my comprehensive exams. In other words, I read the Twilight books when I should have been tearing through Gothic novels and dissecting Romantic-era poems, including Byron's. I mean, I did all that stuff too, but at night I curled up with Bella and Edward as my escape and guilty pleasure. Joke's on me, though, because I was curling up with Gothic novels, and escaping into the fantasy of falling in love with Byron.

There I was, newly married and living in a little rental house near campus that I found totally overwhelming, with the daunting quest of "becoming an expert" ahead of me. At one point, a friend of mine visited, and we watched the first Twilight movie together on the couch. She had just been through a bad breakup, and that impromptu visit had all the hallmarks of a a movie montage: baking apple pies and hugging baby goats and taking pilgrimages to cider presses. At the time it felt like she was sad and I was stressed and we were doing some fun autumnal things in spite of her big feelings and my overwhelming workload, but looking back at the Polaroids I see how young we truly were, and how profoundly we were trying to peel back the layers and figure out the world and our place in it. Is it any surprise we were obsessed with that season's popular Gothic narratives, or that those narratives invited us to conflate falling in love with the quest to subdue the monster?

Inspired by my newfound Twilight addiction and realizing that it would probably be relatable to my students, I designed my next introduction to writing and literature course around the topic of vampires. This was a long time ago—2009, I think—and the sparkle magic vampire craze was in full swing. I had one hipster student who was in it for *Nosferatu* but otherwise that class was pretty much Twilight girls all the way down. I'm talking Twilight girls majoring in hard sciences who had one humanities credit to burn and were using it on this class. I was teaching *Twilight* and the students were, quite literally, there for it.

But first, they would have to read *Dracula*.

Now, let me be clear. I never want to imply that *Dracula* is some masterpiece of protofeminist fiction. If it's anything, I think it's the scariest book ever written about a typewriter. (Part of the premise of *Dracula* is that Mina Harker is compiling the different characters' perspectives in a typeset manuscript, making the typewriter implicitly a subject of the book and thus showing how *technology itself is haunted*.) Bram Stoker might have spent years researching Eastern European history and folklore, but at heart the world *Dracula* comments on is very much the world of late-nineteenth-century London (and maybe also Dublin, as Stoker had Irish roots and was deeply influenced by Irish Gothic writers such as J. Sheridan Le Fanu, whom you might remember from our discussion of his lesbian vampire novella, *Carmilla*). The monster Dracula is a prism you can turn to reveal broad cultural anxieties of Stoker's own moment, such as the fear of immigrants or fear of homosexuality or simply fear of the other. Like most Gothic novels, *Dracula* is more subversive than it is progressive, so it's not even clear whether the novel offers a cogent or coherent rebuttal against those fears—it's more interested in making metaphors about cultural anxiety than in taking a stand against, say, xenophobia. All of this is to say that I'm not claiming *Dracula* is some

Meet a Darcy

NAME:	Edward Cullen
LOVE STORY:	*Twilight*
TURN-ONS:	Sexy blood smells
TURN-OFFS:	The idea of putting someone he loves in danger

You've dated nice guys, and you've dated bad boys, but have you ever dated an immortal monster who glitters in the sun like a Lisa Frank Trapper Keeper? If not, you might want to slide into Edward Cullen's DMs. He's telepathic, with superhuman speed and strength. His eyes change color like a mood ring, and he's never been as drawn to anyone as he is to you. Could he be the vampire of your dreams?

If you're looking for a teen heartthrob, nobody has better practice than Edward, who has been seventeen for, well, a while. He sees you when you're sleeping, he knows when you're awake, and even though you smell delicious to him, you can trust that he won't hurt you. Right?

touchstone of politically admirable thought.

Compared to *Twilight*, though, it is woke as fuck.

Setting aside for a moment all of the gay triangulation in *Dracula*—you know, like the part where all the men give the same girl transfusions of their blood and then talk about how they're all married because their blood is mingling inside her—students in that initial vampire class found the novel appealingly modern in its understanding of feminine identity. I've taught *Dracula* approximately nine million times since then, but that was the only time I also assigned *Twilight*, and students have never again claimed *Dracula* as a girl-power text, which makes me think this interpretation came out of the contrast.

In particular, students in that long-ago course were interested in feminine doubling. The tragic heroine who ends up destroyed in *Dracula* is Lucy Westenra. Monster narratives regularly conflate fear and desire, allowing forbidden desires to come into the light and then pushing those desires right back into the darkness. So Lucy is at once a heroine and a monster, and is simultaneously destroyed and redeemed. We first meet her through her letters to her friend Mina and we learn she is juggling the affections of three suitors—though she doesn't lead anybody on and her choice is clear. Dracula wants a piece of her, too, and the eccentric doctor Van Helsing is committed to saving her, so we find ourselves in a bit of a love hexagon. And Lucy is our hexa-gone girl. She chooses her spouse—gentle aristocrat Arthur Holmwood—but then she's literally eaten alive by the attention she's attracted. In lieu of taking Lucy on as his Victorian-style wife (or "angel in the house," as one nauseating but famous Victorian poem puts it), Arthur has to save her soul. Instead of consummating their love marriage, he has to thrust a stake through her heart. The plight of Lucy's consumption, transformation, demise, and salvation make space in the novel for a new type of it girl, a character at once decidedly modern yet deeply Victorian in her desire to be of devoted service to the men around her. I'm talking about Mina Harker, amanuensis to the stars, who will function as a medium in two senses of the word. First, by compiling the narrative so that the team of monster hunters can, quite literally, get on the same page, and, second, by channeling Dracula's experience and therefore revealing clues to his location after he assaults her. This assault joins Mina and the monster, against her will, in an occult embrace.

When my students realized that *Twilight*'s heroine, the incredibly flat and thus infinitely relatable girl next door Bella Swan, was more a Lucy than a Mina, they were *livid*. And when they realized the closest thing *Twilight* had to *Dracula*'s plucky Mina was the vampire Alice, they wanted a word. Was *Twilight* suggesting that, to have any agency over the plot, a woman had to become a monster? What about the work that *Dracula* had done, they asked, or that feminism had done, to give us permission to root for a heroine who takes matters into her own hands? Why this return to wide-eyed passivity? To sleeping while a creeper watches you? To feeling, when he leaves, that your life has lost all color, all meaning? To being willing to completely and utterly change, right down to your soul, for the chance to be with a monster? Why had they eaten this shit up with a spoon?

In a 2011 essay titled "Our Bella, Ourselves" that was published on the *Hairpin*, English professor Sarah Blackwood explains that her students object to eighteenth-century novels that lack strong heroines. Their misgivings, she says, "sound a lot like the complaints I hear about the *Twilight Saga*. . . . Spending a lot of time in bed, on couches, and being carried around by burly boys, Bella is passive to the point of immobility. Her great love Edward is a controlling stalker, and the novels appear to extol the virtues of abstinence, teen marriage, and feminine 'purity.'" Comparing Bella to more active and self-actualized heroines such as *The Hunger Games*'s Katniss Everdeen, Blackwood writes that "Bella Swan, by contrast, is a much more honest (though cringe-inducing) representation of adolescence. She doesn't know who she is or what she wants. She's clumsy, obtuse, and aggravating in her helplessness. She is also entirely internal, almost alienatingly so." As an example, Blackwood cites the moment in *New Moon* when Edward leaves and Stephenie Meyer inserts a bunch of blank pages to account for the extent to which the beloved monster's absence makes everything feel like a void for Bella.

When the last Twilight book, *Midnight Sun*—a retelling of the original trilogy from Edward's perspective—came out in 2020, I couldn't hit the order button fast enough. I was craving the nostalgic comfort that a cozy Gothic can bring; early in the COVID-19 pandemic, my husband and I had lost our lease unexpectedly and were living, working, and parenting from my childhood home. Perhaps I thought another Twilight book would shift my mood back to a time when the world felt less broken, more full of potential. (My husband and I had gone as Bella and Edward for Halloween in 2009, though he refused to be anointed with glitter and I'd just worn an American Apparel sweatshirt.) When the book arrived, though, I couldn't get into it. I complained about this to my mom, and she said, "right, because who cares about his perspective?"

Well, nobody—and then again, everybody who's bought into the Darcy myth, who believes that winning over the hard-hearted love interest is the ultimate victory. And what's more, I think Meyer might know it. Consider this passage from *Midnight Sun*, in which Edward perches in a tree and watches Bella reading in her backyard:

> She spread the blanket on the damp grass and then lay on her stomach and started flipping through the worn, obviously often-read book, trying to find her place. I read over her shoulder.
>
> Ah—more classics. *Sense and Sensibility*. She was an Austen fan. . . . She read quickly, crossing and recrossing her ankles in the air. I knew the book, so I did not read along with her. Instead, I was watching the sunlight and

wind playing in her hair when her body suddenly stiff-
ened, and her hand froze on the page. . . . She grabbed
a thick section of the book and shoved it roughly over,
almost as if something on the page had angered her. But
what? It was early in the story, just setting up for the first
conflict between mother-in-law and daughter-in-law.
The main hero, Edward Ferrars, was introduced. . . .
I thought through the previous chapter, searching for
something potentially offensive in Austen's overly polite
prose. What could have upset her?

She stopped on the title page for *Mansfield Park*. Beginning a new story—the book was a compilation of novels.

We need to break this down, I think. Edward Cullen, sexy vampire masquerading as a high school student, is one hundred percent
stalking his crush. He's trying to breathe through his nose so he can
ignore the monstrous nature of his visceral attraction, which is, in
this case, the desire to consume and destroy her. At this particular moment—a moment in which she is completely unaware of his
presence—he is *reading Jane Austen over her shoulder*. Austen's marriage
plots here thus provide literal cover for monstrosity. Edward can
read over Bella's delicious shoulder and wonder what in "Austen's
overly polite prose" might have upset her, but the situational irony
is clear. What is truly upsetting is that Bella is being watched by a
predator.

But something in *Mansfield Park* bothers Bella, too: "She'd only
made it to page seven—I was following along this time; Mrs. Norris
was detailing the danger of Tom and Edmund Bertram not encoun-
tering their cousin Fanny Price until they were all adults—when
Bella's teeth ground together and she slammed the book shut."
She falls asleep, muttering "Edmund," and Edward descends into
self-hatred and gloom, imagining her pining for this Edmund Ber-

tram guy: "She wasn't dreaming of me at all, I realized blackly. The self-loathing returned in force. She was dreaming of fictional characters. Perhaps that had always been the case, and all along her dreams had been filled with Hugh Grant in a cravat. So much for my conceit."

OK so, first of all, Stephenie Meyer has clearly not read *Mansfield Park*. She just hasn't. Because Edmund is not Bella's type, and honestly, he's not anybody's type. The rake Henry, I'd allow, but Edmund? Fanny's uptight cousin who is kind but condescending to her, then rejects the girl he's attracted to (and, I would argue, loves) based on some stringent critique of her moral righteousness, and then sort of defaults into marrying his cousin instead? Absolutely not. (Unless, Stephenie, that choice was intentional. Unless you are trying to say that what turns Bella on is the idea of virtue, that what's hot about Edward Vampire is his ability to control his dark desires, like, you know, the one to eat her, which could be boiled down to "the idea of virtue but make it dirty." And unless all the vampires passing as siblings but actually being adults who fuck each other is some exploration of the Romantic-era incest plot, which has deep Gothic roots and has taken meandering literary-historical routes through the history of vampire fiction, and you're, like, alluding to that here. If that's what's going on I owe you an apology and I probably owe you other apologies, too. Have your people call my people.)

But let's put aside my complex feelings about *Mansfield Park* to talk about Edward's complex feelings about Austen. Edward is a monster; he tells the reader, here, that he feels shame about his monstrosity. Not enough shame to stop stalking his crush, mind you; just enough shame not to step into the light. He's jealous and resentful of Bella's book boyfriends, because from his perspective they are teaching her to love the easy and forthright, leading her away from the starkness and darkness of the world and to the sanitized romance of a compilation of classic novels. Joke's on Edward, though, because the Darcy myth is a monster's best ally. What Bella may actually be learning is that even a guy who wants to eat you probably just needs your love.

Indeed, if we trace this passage in *Midnight Sun* back to the original moment in *Twilight*, we find that Bella's engagement with Austen's love interests is not as blithe as the vampire might imagine:

> I lay on my stomach, crossing my ankles in the air, flipping through the different novels in the book, trying to decide which would occupy my mind the most thoroughly. My favorites were *Pride and Prejudice* and *Sense and Sensibility*. I'd read the first most recently, so I started *Sense and Sensibility*, only to remember after I began chapter three that the hero of the story happened to be named *Edward*. Angrily, I turned to *Mansfield Park*, but the hero of that piece was named *Edmund*, and that was just too close. Weren't there any other names available in the late eighteenth century? I snapped the book shut, annoyed, and rolled over onto my back. . . . I pulled all my hair over my head, letting it fan out on the quilt above me, and focused again on the heat that touched my eyelids, my cheekbones, my nose, my lips, my forearms, my neck, soaked through my light shirt . . .

Read back through its refraction in the perspective-flipped retelling, it's hard not to see how Meyer eroticizes the sleeping teenager, who splays herself out like a sacrifice to the monster's gaze. He won't touch her yet but the sun will, and if she dreams of Hugh Grant in a cravat, she does so because he plays a character that shares a name with the monster. Her moment, then, is infused with signifiers and symbols of Edward's presence but she doesn't realize he's really there, watching her.

But I don't know, maybe I'm wrong. I mean, Edward is an immortal vampire, so maybe he knows something I don't—namely, what women want. Maybe, inspired by the connection of his name to Edward Cullen's, Bella really is having a sexy dream about a dry Austen hero. Maybe what she really wants is the love story, the romance plot; maybe the monster narrative is just something that *happens* to her. Maybe Bella really is dreaming about Edmund because Sexy Dreams of Edmund equals Sexy Dreams of the Rules Personified—and that's a slick transition to the *Twilight* fanfic *Fifty Shades of Grey*, the film adaptation of which I am now streaming without headphones in the middle of campus because I need to pull some quotes and my headphones don't work with my work computer, which is my robot nemesis and hates me.

In *Fifty Shades of Grey*'s initial meet-not-exactly-cute, the Bella-based character, Anastasia, shows up to interview the Edward-based Christian about his business success for her school paper. While Twilight's Bella is a high-school student often caught with a weathered copy of a nineteenth-century novel in her hand (the works of Jane Austen, or *Wuthering Heights*), Anastasia is an undergrad English major who carries around her literary perceptions of the world. In this early scene, a telling moment yokes the film's dark effulgence straight to the Darcy myth. Anastasia has been awkward and the interview questions borrowed from her roommate have been too prying. Christian asks her, "What about you? Why don't you ask me something that you want to know?" Anastasia replies, "Earlier, you said that there are some people who know you well. Why do I get the feeling that that is not true?" It's a moment of monstrous connection, the bad boy told he can come into the light, but only with the Belle figure, the bookish shiny-haired brunette who can save him. In response to this moment of emotional excavation, Christian Grey cancels his next meeting and tells Anastasia he can be her Darcy.

CHRISTIAN: I would like to know more about you.

ANASTASIA: There's really not much to know about me.

CHRISTIAN: You said you're an English major? Tell me, was it Charlotte Brontë, Jane Austen, or Thomas Hardy who first made you fall in love with literature?

ANASTASIA: Hardy.

CHRISTIAN: I would have guessed Jane Austen.

Now, I don't know how self-aware this moment is, but we *need* to unpack it. On one level, the joke here is that Anastasia is revealing her depth (she likes Victorian realist fiction, she's invested in tragic characters, she's aware of systemic injustice) while Christian is saying he took her for a romantic. "I would have guessed Jane Austen," then, becomes a pitch-perfect moment of teasing flirtation. And the moment gets echoed later—on their first coffee date, Anastasia mentions that her mother is an incurable romantic. Christian asks if she too is a romantic, and she replies, "Well, I study English lit, so I kind of have to be." Christian's prior mention of Jane Austen proves to have been a test—he ends the date prematurely, convinced he can't be with Anastasia if she's looking for a straightforward love story.

But that moment when Christian Grey mentions Jane Austen— not even ten minutes into the movie, which I apologize for referring to, earlier, as a film—he's not just flirting with her and testing her. He's also calling out the game she's playing. Because while Anastasia might literally fall on her face walking into his fancy office, she knows what she's doing. When she says she gets the feeling people don't really know him, she's offering to be the one to get to know him—to get him, and to know him. She's inviting him to come into the light. And by taking her for a Janeite, Christian is letting her know that he sees what she's doing. After all, isn't he high and mighty and impenetrable? Isn't she asking him to be her Darcy? There's really not much to know about her yet, because meeting him is the first page of her story.

But what kind of story is Anastasia's? What does it mean to be understood, and what does it mean to give yourself away? What does it mean to chain yourself to someone, and what does it mean to let them tie you up? What does it mean to be dominated physically, or to let yourself dominate someone else emotionally? I'm not an expert on any of these topics. I'm just one hundred percent sure the whole thing is about having sex with Byron.

Byron's weird, fragmentary long poem, "The Giaour," assembles pieces of texts from different perspectives to tell a twisted, confusing tale of a woman's murder and how it is avenged by her lover, the eponymous Giaour. The woman had been enslaved and attempts to escape, which leads to her death. Musing on the Giaour's "crime" in avenging the murder, one of the poem's narrators dwells on the theme of vampirism:

> But first, on earth as Vampire sent,
> Thy corse [corpse] shall from its tomb be rent;
> Then ghastly haunt thy native place,
> And suck the blood of all thy race,
> There from thy daughter, sister, wife,
> At midnight drain the stream of life;
> Yet loathe the banquet which perforce
> Must feed thy livid living corse;
> Thy victims ere they yet expire
> Shall know the daemon for their sire,
> As cursing thee, thou cursing them,
> Thy flowers are wither'd on the stem.

I mean, hot, right? Like, you can totally see why that poet would be *the* sex symbol of the early nineteenth century. I'm just kidding, of course, but I wanted to leave you with this moment from sexy historical vampire inspiration Byron himself because I'm interested in how it imagines vampirism as punishment. While "The Giaour" is a very complex and troubling text overall, if we simply zoom in on this monstrous moment and take it on its own terms, we see that Byron, or at least one of the poem's many narrators, suggests that the worst part of being a monster is having the people closest to you *know* you're a monster ("Thy victims ere they yet expire / Shall know the daemon for their sire").

But if both monster narratives and love stories in the Darcy mode hinge on discovering the truth about someone, then how can you know what you're getting into in the first place? And what do we do if the tropes we've constructed surrounding romance allow monsters to hide in plain sight?

Meet a Darcy

NAME:	Christian Grey
LOVE STORY:	*Fifty Shades of Grey*
TURN-ONS:	Domination, legality
TURN-OFFS:	Love and commitment

Look, maybe you just really love a man in an expensive suit, but you also want to get tied up every now and again. Is that too much to ask for? If this sounds familiar, Christian Grey might be the man for you.

Now, let me be clear. In forging his successful veneer, this hottie has overcome a *lot* of trauma. And if love is ever going to be in the cards, you're going to need to be that very special ingenue who is able to peel back his layers to find and parent the scared child within. But in the meantime, he'd like to flick you with a riding crop. If this sounds like your cup of espresso, then hop in the helicopter, because you're in for one exciting ride.

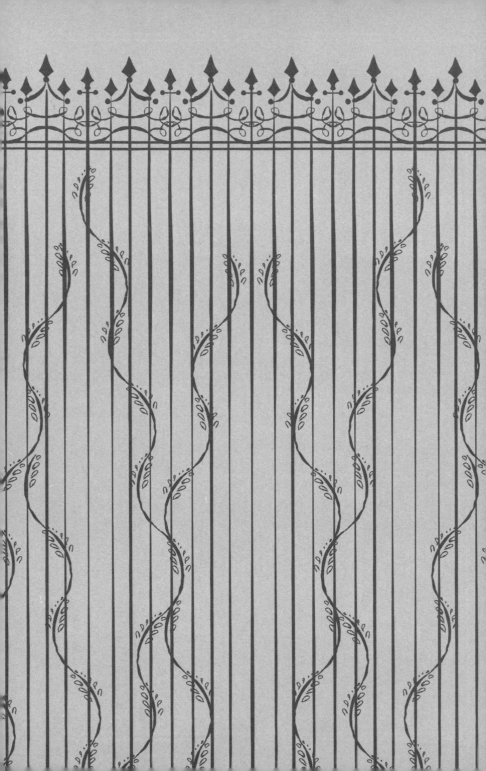

10

Darcy

EVER
AFTER

or, Maybe This Is All the

Fault of Fairy Tales

*T*he Darcy myth not only leads us to value traits in a potential partner that can be dangerous—like mystery and difficulty—but in fact specifically provides cover for that danger. When we're taught that the search for love and the quest to subdue the monster are one and the same, we create a world in which monsters are seen as deserving the benefit of the doubt. By the time we realize we're dealing with a monster, it may be too late.

Austen's classic mystery man, Mr. Darcy, provides this cover on at least two levels. As one of the most famous romantic interests in the history of Western literature, Darcy helped codify the dominant expectation that potential romantic partners—especially heterosexual men—are not only still eligible but in fact *more* appealing when they play a little hard to get, even if playing hard to get involves cruelty, insults, expressions of disinterest, ruining your beloved sister's chances of happiness, and other red flags. Within the world of the novel, Mr. Darcy provides cover for danger in more literal ways. First, his own pride and his understandable desire to protect his sister's reputation (in a world where a woman's reputation plus her monetary resources equals her worth) let Wickham move among people, including vulnerable girls, who don't know he's a rake. Second, and more directly, Darcy ultimately provides Lydia and Wickham with the financial resources that coerce Wickham to go through with the marriage. Sure, this "saves" the Bennet family and makes Lydia respectable again, but it also provides further cover for the monster. Wickham is really a predator and extortionist, but to the general public he just looks like somebody's husband.

While the Darcy myth is dangerous, recognizing its danger doesn't necessarily make Mr. Darcy any less appealing. The tension between Darcy's nefarious cultural influence (as an icon) and morally complex actions (as a fictional character) and his unquenchable smolder are part of what make him—as both an ideal and an archetype—so persistent. (He's not a vampire *exactly*, and yet he never seems to die.)

As I mulled over these questions, I realized that my argument was haunted by something my friend Nan Z. Da said about *Pride and Prejudice* years ago, when we were young and her daughter was small. It seemed like a good time to circle back, so I wrote to her.

ME: OK, so a while back you said something to the effect of, "I don't want my daughter to think taciturn men are Darcys when they turn out to be assholes." When you have a moment can you elaborate?

NAN: Sure. The idea that negging [that is, picking on people] is a sign of burning, suppressed passion is a generic desire, one that believes in infinite reformability. Taciturn men who pick out flaws tend to be that way forever. The boy who pulls your hair at school doesn't actually like you. The fact that you can secure a marriage by insisting otherwise doesn't change those facts. *Pride and Prejudice*'s compensatory and reparative approaches to male abusiveness are part of a revolutionary package of feeling because the time it takes for Lizzy and Darcy to iterate to this desire is the exact amount of time it takes for the landed gentry to level with the aristocracy. I'm not saying Darcy is an asshole but that this path is narrow and non-replicable.

ME: Given that we live in America in the 2020s where all ideas of romance are inflected by what I'm calling the Darcy myth, how do you go about teaching your daughter otherwise? Advising your friends otherwise? Navigating your own relationship to romantic tropes? Do you have an antidote better than mine, which is basically: remember *Wuthering Heights*!

NAN: [Literary theorist Lauren] Berlant said that the typical female complaint is that women live for love and love is the gift that keeps on taking. Knowing that generic desires are abusive doesn't change anything because what else is there? My advice is to know that the length of a book is not the length of your life. You can do a Darcy between breakfast and brunch, feel those thrills, and move on.

I mean, clearly if Nan and I are the mice in the '90s cartoon *Pinky and the Brain*, I'm Pinky. But cartoon mice aside, I'm low-key obsessed with this idea of "doing a Darcy." It doesn't sound like advice one would give to their teenage daughter but I think Nan means it. But is this just cool-mom pragmatism, or does it buy into the Darcy myth anyway, Swiftie style? Does the suggestion to "do a Darcy" between breakfast and brunch suggest that dealing with a Darcy who turns out to be a rake in disguise is not that bad after all, or won't have a particularly damaging effect on one's life? That as long as our *expectation* isn't a real-deal romantic hero, we can still hold the upper hand while dealing with the ersatz Darcys all around us? (Also, now I want every day to include both breakfast and brunch.)

In response to my mention of *Wuthering Heights* as an antidote to the Darcy myth, Nan wrote: "Yes, seriously remember *Wuthering Heights*. Look for signs of animal abuse!" I wasn't even thinking about the part of *Wuthering Heights* where Heathcliff hangs up a dog by her collar, but Nan's cautionary note took me back to a moment when I was younger and a woman I knew confided that a former boyfriend had poisoned her dog. How many of these stories do we hear and tuck away somewhere? Remember eighteenth-century author Eliza Haywood, whose novels encouraged women to go out and live life, knowing life was dangerous? In her 1751 novel *The History of Miss Betsy Thoughtless*, the heroine, Betsy, receives a pet squirrel from one of her many suitors. Betsy cherishes and cares for the squirrel, but her husband—not the same man who gave her the squirrel—throws it against the marble chimney with the whole force of his strength, killing it and, as he tells Betsy, saving the expense of its upkeep. This violent act is meant to remind Betsy that she is her husband's personal property, and only worthy of his tenderness so long as she obeys (and so long as her lifestyle is not too costly).

Now, I am not calling Mr. Darcy a squirrel murderer! But the fact that Jane Austen traced literary history back through the Gothic to the realistic (and moralistic) stylings of Haywood and company is very telling. Perhaps Nan's take on Lizzy and Darcy's love hits the mark. Perhaps *Pride and Prejudice* is a fable, a story with a moral. Or perhaps it is a fairy tale, a path "narrow and non-replicable" (as Nan put it) through the dark forest of our fears, even if this Gothic landscape is overlaid with a gilded version of the "real" world. Perhaps, inspired by Darcy and his ilk, we've been trying to love beasts hard enough to turn them into princes, when all along we should have been remembering that most beasts are *not* in fact princes, that magic isn't real, that this fantasy should function as fantasy alone. Perhaps "reformability" is a made-up word, just as the idea that you can fix a problematic partner is a concept made up to train you to date him even though he treats you like dirt.

Indeed, it's quite possible that Austen might have been influenced by fairy tales as well as Gothic terror. While stories about fairies and supernatural creatures are in general an older, oral form, in England the types of tales we would call fairy tales today were very much an eighteenth- and early nineteenth-century invention. Scholar Elizabeth Wanning Harries argues that the history of fairy tales in England is really a history of translation. While an English translation of Grimm's stories wasn't published in England until the 1820s, a translation of Charles Perrault's tales (including some of the best-known early versions of the Cinderella and Little Red Riding Hood stories) appeared in 1729; along with other early translations of fairy tales, it was influential to eighteenth-century fiction. For example, Alicia Kerfoot (also a literary scholar) has noticed a possible Cinderella reference in Samuel Richardson's 1740 novel *Pamela*, a rags-to-riches tale we know Jane Austen read: Pamela loses a shoe heel. What this connection might show is that English translations of fairy tales were affecting British literary history, whether people were making deliberate references or just affected by a fairy tale zeitgeist. Sarah Fielding's 1749 work *The Governess*, an early example of didactic children's literature, includes original stories written in the style of fairy tales. We can also think about how fairy tales might have influenced the Gothic novel, infusing the mysterious, natural scenes and dark dilemmas of the Gothic with a sense of storied history and the mythic literary past. Since we know English translations of fairy tales influenced eighteenth-century literature, it's probable that they influenced Jane Austen, at least indirectly. As an avid reader with access to her father's impressive library, it's also quite likely that Jane Austen encountered Robert Samber's 1729 English translation of Perrault's tales in youth or even early childhood, as well.

And fairy tales bring us right back to the figure of the rake. Samber's translation of "The Little Red Riding Hood" concludes with a "moral" for "growing ladies fair." That moral is essentially: stay away from rakes. "Wolves too sure there are / Of every sort, and every character," the moral reads, including some who are "tame, familiar, full of complaisance," and who use "language wondrous sweet" to hide their intentions even as they leeringly follow young women around. These "simpering Wolves," the story concludes, are even more dangerous than their vicious animal counterparts. Human men can sweet-talk and dissemble. They are artful, educated in the ways of the world. They are capable of hiding their designs, skilled in the art of deception. They are able to follow a growing girl from a chance encounter in the street to the very edge of her bed.

What if we read *Pride and Prejudice* as a play on Little Red Riding Hood? As a British soldier, it is the rake Wickham who wears red. He's enchanting to converse with; he's after young ladies. Lizzy doesn't go with him, but Lydia does. If *Pride and Prejudice* is a fairy tale, maybe that's the point. Lizzy's union with her Prince Charming has less to do with Darcy himself and more to do with some universal logic that rewards her for avoiding the beast in disguise. Lydia gets eaten by a wolf whereas Lizzy gets her happily ever after.

Darcy might be Lizzy's reward for avoiding the rake, but the Darcy myth also tempts us to walk right into the rake's trap, offering rewards if we take a gamble on a guy who seems like bad news and guess correctly that he's really a prince in disguise. We're still dealing with the consequences of that storyline today.

For instance, let's fast-forward *really* far, from the 1729 translation of Charles Perrault to the fall of 2022, when we were all briefly very interested in Adam Levine's bad sexts. Instagram model and influencer Sumner Stroh, of whom I had never previously heard, went viral for posting a video in which she leaked private Instagram messages from Maroon Five front man Adam Levine suggesting they'd had an affair. In the video, Stroh claimed that a friend was attempting to sell the story of her affair to a tabloid, which is why she was coming forward herself. In a follow-up video, Stroh went on to explain that, at the time of their affair, she was under the impression that Levine's marriage to Victoria's Secret model Behati Prinsloo was over—a lie that, she tells her hundreds of thousands of followers, she believed because she was young, naïve, easily manipulated, and new to the scene in LA. She was thus exploited, she tells us, her morals unknowingly compromised.

The occasion for the video—or, the occasion for Stroh discussing the affair with some friends whom she thought she trusted—is a bizarre message Stroh claims to have received from Levine. The text reads, "Ok serious question. I'm having another baby and if it's w [*sic*] boy I really wanna name it Sumner. You ok with that? DEAD serious." He follows this up with a shrug emoji.

Stroh tells us she is in hell, and honestly, it's pretty cringey. I mean, naming your baby after your mistress is bad enough—but only if it's a boy? It's almost as if Levine expects Stroh to have no subjectivity whatsoever. (Levine denied the affair but didn't deny that the DMs were from him, and other women almost immediately came forward to share their own cringey extramarital sexts from Levine.)

Now, I am not here to judge anybody (or everybody). I am here to talk about the difference between being *told* a fairy tale and being *sold* a fairy tale.

Was Stroh sold a fairy tale by Levine? We can't really know, but if we take her at her word, we get a bit of a Darcy myth gone wrong: the tall, dark, by some accounts handsome, rich celebrity figure telling you that nobody really knows his marriage is over, but you're special, and you understand, and also you're hot. Stroh said that Levine was "hiding in plain sight" by using his verified Instagram account to flirt with her. After all, if he were really trying to conceal his communications with other women from his wife, wouldn't he choose a more ephemeral, private way to be in touch? But really it's the Darcy myth that lets the rake hide in plain sight. If romantic heroes are often rude, withholding, insulting, or shady before you love them into submission, then it stands to reason that rude, withholding, insulting, or shady guys just need some time to blossom. Stroh explains that Levine knew she believed everything he said.

I am told that Levine is, or at least was, a self-professed "wife guy," a category whose boundaries are a little mushy but that basically means a man who uses his overt, vocal devotion to his wife to upgrade his social standing, public persona, or social media fame. It may not be a coincidence that several prominent wife guys (comedian John Mulaney, YouTube personality Ned Fulmer) have had very visible cheating scandals and/or divorces in recent years. And it's worth asking how the wife guy archetype relates to the Darcy myth. Both present an idealized hetero love match in which a particular woman is valorized. However, the lionization of the "wife" offers a gentle, compassionate face for what is really a patriarchal concept:

cashing in your woman for social and/or cultural capital. And both the Darcy myth and the wife guy archetype create cultural vacuums in which rakes can prey on their victims in plain sight, and women who don't adhere to societal expectations are left ruined. (Although this isn't the nineteenth century, and, at least for professional influencers, there's a lot of overlap between being ruined and being made.) Basically what I'm saying is that marriage plots can also be monster narratives. And that I wish Lydia Bennet had had TikTok.

In one of her videos, Sumner Stroh says that "being naïve is not an excuse for what I did," and maybe that is what the Darcy myth tell us, but it is a double-edged sword. You shouldn't be naïve, you should know how the world works. You should know, as my students once chirped in unison, to watch out for Wickhams. And yet the fairy tale that teaches you how to keep your eyes peeled for wolves also shows you a safe path through the woods that was never really there. His name is Mr. Darcy, and he is a promise the patriarchy will break again and again and again.

PART THREE

Our Darcys,

OURSELVES

11

Darcys of
OUR LIVES

or, The Healing
Power of Gossip

Your life isn't being controlled by a room full of writers scarfing down takeout while they discuss where your character arc should go next, but sometimes it sure feels like it. This could be (at least in part) because we have Darcy on the brain.

I asked some friends and acquaintances to share their real-life Darcy experiences with me. Almost everybody I asked said that the Darcy trope resonated with them in some way, and had a story to share. One interviewee even told me that her therapist has affirmed my sense that everyone who has loved and lost has loved a Darcy at some point.

Jen (all the names in this chapter have been changed) is a long-married woman in her late forties who works for a law firm in a major US city. A while back, she found herself crossing paths with a colleague who annoyed her. Jason was an arrogant asshole, so it struck her as the "weirdest thing" when she found herself attracted to him, even developing a crush.

Jen decided to process her feelings with her longtime therapist. This therapist, who knew about Jen's lifelong love of literature, told her that she was having a "Mr. Darcy experience." Jen remembers that, in their session, her therapist told her that she should not be surprised but should in fact expect to have experiences like these. The therapist shared her theory that every romance is a romance with Mr. Darcy in some form, that everyone loves Mr. Darcy and that every single love story conforms to the Mr. Darcy story in some way. With a surprised laugh, Jen told me that her therapist went so far as to claim that if you think the love story you're in doesn't conform to the Darcy archetype, you're either lying to yourself or experiencing some other version of Darcy that doesn't look the way you might expect. According to her therapist, Jen tells me, the initial dislike Jen felt for Jason was part of the story.

I reached out to Jen's therapist for comment and, while she couldn't discuss her patients with me, she did admit that she talks about Darcy with mostly single women more than one might think, and certainly more than any other literary character.

Jen said that her understanding of her therapist's point was two-fold. First, she thought her therapist was implying that there was something satisfying about the frisson of clashing with someone while knowing that interactions with that person could feel positive down the line. Second, Jen took her therapist to mean that lots of stories that *aren't* great love stories also follow the Darcy pattern—but that following the pattern is the thing that makes them feel like love. In this case, Jen's crush on Jason eventually came to feel ridiculous to her. It was just a work crush, not something she was going to pursue or someone she was going to fall in love with, and it certainly wasn't a threat to her marriage. Even so, Jen was left scratching her head, wondering what it was about having a moment of initial dislike with a man she saw as arrogant that activated sexual and romantic attraction for her. In other words, why did finding somebody annoyingly arrogant translate so quickly, in her mind, into a crush?

Jay, a queer person in their early sixties, is a longtime lover of Jane Austen, and so had a lot of self-awareness during their Mr. Darcy experience. Jay told me that, in general, they know they have "a pattern of quite strong hostile first response to overbearing people, followed by unexpectedly finding myself attracted to them." Jay explained that "the Darcy pattern is unhelpful for me because it suggests that I shouldn't trust my first impressions, that a strong initial dislike is the start of romance—when in fact I need to recognize that there's a good reason I had this response to that person. It's easy to see in hindsight that they were not a good person for me to be involved with, but actually SOMETHING WAS ALREADY TELLING ME AND I IGNORED IT/OVERRODE IT. In my unhappier moments I think that my subsequent attraction to these people—who tend to be very critical and lay down the law about everything—is a form of submission/wanting approval, and I don't like that."

Within this framework, the Darcy moment Jay tells me about

makes them laugh out loud. Years ago, when they were in their early forties, Jay found themselves thrown together frequently with a friend of their partner at the time; I'll call this person Chaz. Jay was wary of Chaz and did not like him at all—but then Chaz moved to a spectacularly beautiful part of France, and invited Jay and their partner to come visit. Upon their arrival in France, Jay described themself as feeling immediately "zapped" with desire for Chaz. Jay ended up having a tryst with Chaz in the car, which "was awful, and messy, and a spectacularly bad idea for so many reasons—but it was also funny, even at the time, because I couldn't help thinking of *Pride and Prejudice*: 'I believe I must date it from my first seeing his beautiful grounds at Pemberley.'" Sometimes what you have a crush on isn't the person in question, per se, but that person's situation—a beautiful home, family wealth, a fancy education, an adventurous life, and so forth. But when seeing someone's attractive life leads you to feel attracted to them, have you actually gained new information, or is it just the context that appeals to you? The fantasy we see in *Pride and Prejudice* is that both of these can happen simultaneously— Pemberley is awe-inspiring, *and also* Darcy's housekeeper raves about him. In reality, however, we need to be careful not to confuse one with the other. Chaz was the same guy he'd always been, just in a new, beautiful location.

Sometimes Darcy lives in a beautiful part of France, and some-times he's renting a Brooklyn apartment the size of a postage stamp. When I asked Abigail to tell me her Mr. Darcy story, she focused on the character's arrogance and insistent gaze. When this particular Darcy encounter took place, Abigail was living in Brooklyn in her midtwenties. Through a mutual friend, Abigail kept crossing paths with a cute guy named Micah. Reflecting on these encounters, Abi-gail told me, "He was always kind of standoffish and seemed too cool for school, but then would sometimes be weirdly attentive to me or give me these knowing glances or whatever. One time we ended up at a bar together and he spent the whole time gossiping to me about his roommate and his roommate's girlfriend in a really snobby way (both of whom were perfectly nice people?)." Abigail reports that, to her knowledge, Micah's former roommate and his then girlfriend are married now, and seem happy. "It was a very, like, Jane isn't good enough for Mr. Bingley situation," Abigail explained.

Then, one night, Micah ended up coming to a party at Abigail's apartment. They drank a bunch of Four Loko (this was the early 2000s) and made out on the roof, and then Abigail went back to his place for a sexual encounter. The next morning, she recalls, "we had coffee and bagels, and walked around the park, and talked about a bunch of stuff, and it was like, yes, I've broken through the curmudgeonly surface to the sweet man beneath! And then he literally never talked to me again, including when we were at a small birthday dinner together and he didn't make eye contact with me the whole time."

This, my friends, is the Darcy myth in a nutshell. Girl meets boy (in this scenario—it's not always going to be a boy, though the Darcy is a masculine role in the sexist way our culture understands romance dynamics). Boy creates a sense of mystery and connection between them. Boy is arrogant and judgmental of others. Boy and girl are thrown together, again and again, by chance. Boy drinks Four Loko! Girl drinks Four Loko! Boy and girl consummate their crush, and girl thinks it's the beginning of something. But Darcy isn't real, that guy was just a horny jerk, and this is the end.

When I first asked if she had ever dated a Darcy figure, Abigail quipped, "Yes, although none of them ever made a turn and professed their love for me." But that's exactly the point. Micah never acted in a way that suggested he would profess his love for Abigail, but the Darcy myth set her up to take that fall. The Darcy myth is a script about love that we run in our heads. While this script might seem fun when we're happily married and bored at work, or when we feel safe and comfortable relating to love and sex in a casual way, it also has the potential to lead us to repeat damaging patterns, cause harm, and get hurt.

Deep Dark Darcy

This is something that Anya, a sales professional in her early thirties, was able to speak to. Anya told me that she's dated men in the past whom she thought she could "fix," but it never worked. She knows now that the person she wanted to be with in these relationships was someone she had made up in her head, and she has a history of giving the real men she's dated credit for her fantasies even while she ignores their red flags.

Anya told me that she has come to terms with the way she sometimes tends to escalate situations in romantic relationships, and explained that she thinks she does this because of behavioral patterns she developed in response to abuse and neglect in childhood. At the same time, Anya reported that when she's dated guys who seem like "bad boys," it often feels like they're running on autopilot, too—talking to her but really speaking past her to their parent, their ex, or another person who hurt them.

But in addition to acting based on past trauma, Anya tells me that some of her ideas about love and romance have also been shaped by popular culture. She especially had words for *Beauty and the Beast,* whose Darcy myth bona fides we've already discussed: "Belle is just nurturing to this beast who is such an asshole, and she bends over backwards to look for the good and makes excuses for his behavior." Learning to walk away from the "bad boy" instead of trying to turn him into a prince, Anya says, was part of reconciling herself to and healing from her past trauma. Anya tells me that, while she has nurturing instincts, she's getting better at focusing on whether a guy is actually right for her or just seems in need of someone who will try to "fix" him.

Darcy experiences don't just trigger learned behavior from past trauma, but can in fact provide cover for traumatic interactions. Faye, a nonbinary person in their early forties, draws parallels between their relationship with their former spouse and an experience of being groomed by an older man in their chosen field when Faye was in their early twenties. In both instances, Faye tells me, they distrusted their initial impressions of the person in question because "some social circle had deemed them important." Doubling down on the way that romance since Darcy has hinged on understanding a potential love interest in light of that person's past, Faye explained that they first "connected" with the man who groomed them "because we had tragic/abusive/complicated father stories." Faye later learned that connecting on the premise of shared, past trauma not only is a romance trope but can actually be a grooming tactic.

While shows like *Gossip Girl* and *Bridgerton* might teach us that a Darcy's own past trauma can be healed by the redemptive power of our love, this is not always the case and can leave us expecting more from ourselves than we are able to deliver. Maria, a now happily engaged woman in her late twenties, tells me that her Mr. Darcy was a guy named Max. They had a slow-burn, will-they-won't-they dynamic pulled straight from the pages of a romance novel and precipitated by a series of meet-cutes. Sometimes Max pretended not to know Maria when he saw her in public; sometimes he commented on Maria's relationship with the man she was dating; sometimes he gave her rides home in the rain. Seeing him made her stomach do flip-flops, which she hated: "I get that stupid jump in my stomach . . . I hate that jump, I hate that I have it over this annoying man . . . I hate him. And I HATE that he makes me feel this way."

Long story short, after months of a clandestine, mutual crush, bolstered by lots of secrecy, jealousy, and competition, Maria finally broke things off with her boyfriend. She ran to Max's apartment, knocked on his door, and kissed him when he opened it, telling him everything. Then she looked behind him into the apartment itself, and saw that Max was in the process of packing up. He was being deployed to Afghanistan.

The pair kept in touch while Max was away, with some ups and downs, but when he came home their love turned tragic. Despite being beautiful and devoted, Maria wasn't able to help Max heal from the traumas he had witnessed and endured while away, and he was never able to fully open up to her. (Perhaps the very notion that being beautiful and devoted qualifies someone to help a partner overcome their trauma is one of the most dangerous lies the Darcy myth perpetuates.) Once they were back in the same city, Max and Maria had a passionate and ultimately explosive affair, which was far from the happily ever after their romance novel trajectory had led Maria to expect. While Max is now a successful and accomplished business owner, Maria says, "I truly fear he is going to never be able to find love until he breaks down that pride he holds on to so tightly." Whether Max and Maria's tumultuous breakup is the fault of his post-traumatic psychological state and the couple's incompatible personalities, or whether it was inevitable from the enemies-to-lovers energy of their first interactions, one thing is certain. Our shared cultural notions of romance dictate that Max should or could have been Maria's great love, when in fact she wound up unable to help him heal, and feeling hurt herself.

Disappearing Darcys

Darcy encounters can be heavy as hell, but they can also be, in the words of one interviewee, "cuckoo bananas." Mei, a woman in her late twenties, tells me that "the one and only time" she's ever been "intrigued by the 'bad boy' or 'arrogant-prick-turned-prince-charming'" was when she was in the waning phase of a nine-year relationship with her high school sweetheart. During this time, Mei found herself sparring, intellectually, with a coworker, Jack. Mei describes Jack as someone who walked the line between being funny and seeming overly full of himself. At first, Mei mostly gave Jack shit for thinking he was clever, but over time they became close. Then, out of nowhere, Jack professed his complete, undying, devoted love for Mei. Mei says that this was totally out of left field, and emotion-

AITA for being "jerk-phobic" against a guy who might like me?

I (F20) met a man (M20s) at a party where he was kind of bad-mouthing my looks behind my back. I overheard this girl who is kinda my frenemy saying that he actually liked me, but every time I spent time with him he was awkward and a little mean. Then I found out that he broke up my sister and her boyfriend on purpose because he thinks our whole family is embarrassing. My friends are all pressuring me to give him another chance, saying I'm being really unfair and biased by assuming that he can't get better. They say if I just help him come out of his shell, he'll turn out to be a great guy, but I'm finding it a little hard to let go of his past actions. Am I the asshole for being so prejudiced?

AITA for doing a huge favor for a girl's family?

I (M28) recently helped a friend (M22) avoid a bad marriage with a girl (F20s) who only wanted him because of his money and because her trashy mom was pressuring her to get married. Now the girl's sister (F19?) is mad at me. I think the sister is kind of cute, not really my type and I've told her so but she has nice eyes, but now that she found out I ruined her sister's wedding she won't give me the time of day. So I secretly paid for her other sister (F16) to marry this guy (M20s) who tried to seduce my sister last year. And I think she's still mad at me??? Not sure what else I could have done here but AITA?

ally confusing for her, as she had begun to feel that she and her boyfriend were at the end of their relationship; suddenly, Jack seemed like an "exit door." Jack started telling Mei constantly that her boyfriend didn't love her anymore and that nobody had ever loved her the way that he did. Jack insisted that he and Mei were meant to be together, and embarked on a love-bombing campaign: buying her thoughtful gifts, walking her home every night, asking her to dinner all the time, drying her tears after stressful days at work, calling and texting her constantly, and begging her to end her relationship so that they could be together. Mei says that she remembers thinking, "Wow! No one has ever cared about me THIS much. I guess this is what's meant to be." She had a conversation with her boyfriend about opening up their relationship, slept with Jack a few times, and then told him she was ready to take the leap and be together.

That's when things took a turn, and Mei almost couldn't believe her ears. She explained: "I reached out to him to tell him that I wanted to try things with him and finally be together . . . and then poof! He tells me he stopped caring about me a long time ago, that he just wasn't really feeling it with me, and proceeded to start to call into question whether he had ever had feelings for me in the first place. I was literally flabbergasted. He completely gaslit me into thinking that he had never been the unbelievably devoted lover straight out of a Jane Austen novel at all."

The story of the Darcy who disappears the minute he gets what he wants should be unusual, but it isn't. Another interviewee, Maggie, spun a very similar yarn when I asked if she had ever dated a Darcy. Maggie is a medical professional in her late thirties who recently got devastating mixed signals from a guy she thought she loved. The Darcy in question, Peter, was a member of her friend group who had repeatedly professed his interest in dating her. Peter had all the makings of a romantic comedy love interest. While he came from a difficult childhood with significant family trauma, he had made his way in the world, accruing success and privilege.

He was a bit of a dream man—sharp intelligence, quirky interests, understated athletic pursuits, a unique but conventionally attractive look, the whole nine yards.

Maggie was hesitant. She wasn't sure if she was ready for something serious, especially within the friend group. But as she and Peter grew closer, her feelings grew. He was consistent and persistent about wanting something more with her, and their friendship began to dip into romantic territory. Peter took Maggie out on clearly delineated dates, and constantly touched and flirted with her. They even had a few steamy moments together when things definitely crossed the line from friends to more-than-friends. The two were in touch constantly, texting all day every day.

Finally, after years of their on-again, off-again friendship/situationship/relationship, having worked to heal her own wounds in response to the strength and persistence of Peter's feelings and professed desire to be with her, Maggie decided it was time to take the plunge. Surely, this was her great love. She bought a plane ticket and flew to meet Peter in another city, where he had been stationed on a short-term work assignment.

That's when things took a turn for the worse. Maggie confessed her love to Peter, and told him she was ready for whatever their future held. But even though she was giving him what she thought he wanted, Peter suddenly lost interest in her. He claimed that Maggie only wanted to be with him because their mutual friends had mostly gotten married, and because he was tall. He pretended to be confused about the idea that there had ever been anything romantic between them. Instead of self-consciously resolving his childhood trauma to forge a loving future with Maggie, as he might have done if he had been a character in a romance novel and not a real person with an avoidant attachment style, Peter seemingly couldn't handle the pressure that came with Maggie confessing her love to him. Instead of embarking on a relationship, he claimed not to have realized she had romantic feelings for him. Instead of embracing

Maggie at the end of their extended will-they-won't-they, Peter went so far as to resent her for taking so long to come around to the idea of being together, essentially saying that, given her age, she should have known how to solidify them as a couple, and should have done it long before her confession. Maggie told me that, even after this tumultuous end to their story, Peter still flirts with her and touches her upper thigh when their mutual friendships put them in the same room. Maggie told me, "By the time I trusted him he was over it, and what's terrible is I still like him and miss his friendship, because he's lovely and horrible."

Let's talk about the Darcy myth, here, because it is a two-way street. By waiting until she truly trusted Peter, Maggie, who had been burned before in a past relationship, was asking him to be Darcy: to be steadfast, to give her a moment to come around, to allow her to grow in love, to prove himself. But Peter wasn't Darcy. We might even understand him as someone after a myth of his own, someone lusting after the person he could not have precisely because he could not have her. (I don't know Peter and I'm not a therapist, but my guess is that this made him feel safe—if someone won't commit to you, then she can never leave you.) Maggie thought that Peter stuck around despite her reticence because he was serious about dating her, when it's very possible that Peter stuck around because he had a bone-deep need to burn, pine, and ache for someone who wouldn't love him and thus couldn't leave him. Similarly, Mei thought that Jack wouldn't give up on her because of the strength of his love, but maybe, for whatever reason, he simply needed to know that he could get what he wanted.

This is exactly the kind of scenario the Darcy myth is engineered to resolve. If Maggie and Peter's story were being devised in the writers' room of *Bridgerton* or *Gossip Girl*, or if it were playing out between the glossy covers of a sexy paperback, we know what would happen next. Peter would realize his mistake, would resolve the childhood trauma that made it difficult to commit to Maggie. He would come and find her, meeting her grand gesture with one of his own. She would forgive him his mistakes, because she knows about his backstory and understands why her confession of love was so triggering to him. They would get together, and stay together.

But the Darcy myth is just that—a myth. Peter didn't change, and Maggie got hurt, and when they cross paths from time to time, he still hits on her. I don't think the message here needs to be, necessarily, that people never change. But just because he seems like your Darcy, it doesn't mean he's going to deliver on the promises the Darcy myth has sold you.

I heard another disappearing Darcy story from Zachary, a gay man in his early thirties. Zachary tells me that, in his late twenties, he dated an older man who stands out as a Darcy to him. This man, Ian, was in his forties, and "played up the emotionally unavailable thing" in their relationship. Despite this, Zachary found that "there was something that attracted me to him—his self-assuredness I suppose?" Zachary says that Ian had a sort of "been there done that ennui," that to Ian everyone seemed an easy, predictable exercise. He was aloof and never shared his emotions. Zachary says that "honestly, that younger me wanted to be worthy of his attention" although he sees that now as "a deep reflection of my insecurities."

Ian ultimately ghosted, which Zachary finds unsurprising. One moment he was in Zachary's life and the next—he wasn't.

When Zachary and I discuss the months he spent dating Ian in terms of the Mr. Darcy archetype, Zachary says that it's "particularly interesting to talk about this very heterosexual archetype and its perverse applicability to gay men." Zachary thinks that since many young, gay men lack access to queer role models and gay elders, heterosexual archetypes like the Darcy myth can, sometimes uncritically, emerge as relationship models. Perhaps these damaging archetypes need to be countered not simply by personal awakenings but also by radical acts of community care. In order to avoid falling into the trap of the disappearing Darcy, we need to see what other models of intimacy are possible. And in order to see successful models of intimacy in a wide variety of relationships, we need to be surrounded by vibrant, supportive, and supported communities.

Our First Darcys

We are fed the Darcy myth from an early age; perhaps unsurprisingly, Darcy experiences were part of several interviewees' romantic education. For example, Kayla, a nonprofit development professional in her early forties, tells me that she dated a Darcy deep in her past. She was young, and he was unbelievably arrogant, a drummer she knew from the music scene. "He felt too sure of himself," she tells me, "and I felt unsure of him because of it." But, she remembers, "he had this way of making me feel like his life wasn't his own doing . . . he had some power over me." Kayla got together with her Darcy even though he had a girlfriend when they met, and even though he never fully released that tumultuous relationship after breaking up with that girlfriend. When we're taught to look for a lover we can "fix," we can sometimes find ourselves wrapped up in their dysfunctional relationship dynamic, with no power to heal it. When Kayla realized that her Darcy's ex was never going to be completely gone from his life, she dumped him. He showed up seven years later to declare his love, but Kayla explained that this made her "cringe" because she had "moved myself and my life so far past this noncommittal cheater." She never saw him again after that.

Maybe we believe we can fix these early Darcys because we're young and naïve—or maybe we're just really good students, and have developed a solid sense of what romance is supposed to look like. When the pop quiz comes, we've studied hard but have learned the wrong answers. Ella tells me about a time when she misinterpreted a Darcy's actions as a profound, romantic gesture. She was in business school, and her crush, Tres, came from a prominent family in the city where she was living. Ella describes Tres as unbelievably handsome and fun, and she was hurt when she learned that he was spending time with her even though he had a girlfriend. She told him not to get in touch with her again, but then he broke up with his girlfriend in order to date her. Ella was blown away to learn that he felt this strongly about her . . . until a week later, when she ran into him at a night club with an underwear model. When Tres broke up with his girlfriend in order to date Ella, it seemed like a grand gesture that had to do with how special he thought she was. But maybe it was actually giving her different information: letting her know that he viewed women as interchangeable and expendable.

Loden and her friend Jade are young, but not naïve. Loden is a fifteen-year-old high school student who recently broke up with her first serious boyfriend. When I asked Loden if her breakup resonated with the Darcy myth, she joked that "unfortunately for me as well as my girlboss She.E.O. anti-patriarchy fantasies, this was a genuinely sweet guy and we broke up because I'd lost feelings." That said, Loden explained, she and her friends have a history of trying to "fix" the guys they like; these romantic prospects generally prove unfixable. Loden traces this desire to fix people to the "huge glorification of the power of female love." She says that she and her friends have been told by society, and especially by romance movies and books, that you can "fix somebody with just, like, your feminine charms" but that the more they have tried and failed, the more they have realized that this is just a fantasy.

Jade, who is eighteen, dated an emotionally immature photographer. He was "a little chap who was insecure" about how he appeared in front of people, and projected that judgmental attitude on relationships, Jade explained. Jade felt that she could make him a less cynical optimist and show him the beauty in everything while earning his love. She was incredibly frustrated when things didn't go that way. In perhaps the most cringey moment imaginable, the guy broke up with her, then pulled out his camera and asked Jade to take a breakup selfie with him. She declined.

Loden told me that, within the self-aware, artsy corner of youth culture that she occupies, enlightenment can be used as a tool to excuse bad behavior. Loden told me that people claim self-growth as a way to avoid taking responsibility for their actions. For example, Loden told me about a guy she was hanging out with for a couple of months. She described him as an indie boy who seemed to believe that his good music taste was a sign of his high emotional intelligence. This guy—let's call him Thom—told Loden that he had "an equal amount of feelings for another girl" and couldn't decide between them. Loden distinctly remembers Thom telling her that he was feeling all his emotions and that he couldn't help but feel things for a lot of people. From Loden's perspective, he seemed to be saying that because he was aware of something negative he was doing, he was fixing it, when in fact he was putting the onus of the situation on her. Loden felt shattered by this, but understood what he was doing and broke things off with him. Making fun of the trend of "performative sensitivity" that she's noticed among the young men that she and her friends date, Loden quipped, "look how redeemable my bad qualities are because I can play the guitar!"

In our discussion of the indie boy trope and her negative experience with a guy like this, Loden mentioned that it's not uncommon to slide into someone's DMs to ask if they listen to Radiohead. I said, "it's still Radiohead? It was Radiohead when I was in high school!" With delicate irony and perfect delivery, Loden said, "it's still Radiohead because there's no good music now so we are just going back to the old people music." Then she quipped, "I'll burn you a CD because I'm so retro and have such good taste," and my bones crumbled into dust and drifted away to join the sands of time.

With crystalline wisdom, Loden wrapped up our conversation by reflecting that young love is the root of perceptions about adult love. I hadn't thought of it this way—perhaps because I've been an adult for so long—but it makes sense, doesn't it? What we learn about love when we're young—whether via experience, or through the messages and stories we consume—has a profound effect on the lives and worlds we build, and on the stories we tell about who we have become.

Just Like Darcy

The Darcy myth sets us up for negative, disappointing, and even traumatic romantic experiences. It does this by training us, through its persistent repetition across different media, that great loves often start with bad first impressions. Our job, according to the Darcy myth, is to overcome our prejudice while learning the truth about the person we dislike; their job is both to reveal themselves to us and to overcome their shortcomings and fix their past mistakes, making themselves better in the sanctifying fire of our love.

Relationships that start out with red flags are going to go wrong a lot of the time. But this doesn't mean that Darcy experiences are always negative. Sometimes they go right, or end up being satisfying in ways we might not expect. Sometimes our experiences with Darcys lead us to a fulfilling relationship with someone else.

Trish, a happily married woman in her forties, had a history of going for "bad boys" before she met her husband. She tells me that her husband is "one of very few non-assholes in my history of dating men" but also mentions that "I think sometimes people think he's an asshole, which probably turns me on." Reflecting on her history of being "prone to obsession with the person who seems not to like anybody," she muses that this dynamic might have to do with wanting to win the admiration of men who are hard to please, thus proving that she is a person who should be taken seriously. In terms of her courtship with her husband, she tells me he "has the unwittingly high standards of an autodidact, and I was absolutely determined to prove I wasn't just some Ivy League princess."

Another interviewee, Rose, tells me about a Darcy experience that ended up with both Rose and her Darcy finding true love—

just not with each other. The Darcy in question, Enzo, was a handsome older man and "cocky asshole" whom she knew through work and through mutual friends. They had a steamy make-out session on the street the night they met, but she wouldn't let him come up to her apartment; this apparently put her alone in the category of women who had rejected his advances, and seducing her became his white whale. Rose and Enzo embarked on a years-long friends-with-benefits situation that felt like a weird romantic movie. (For example, Enzo asked Rose to be his plus-one at a dinner with his coupled-up friends, then kissed her behind a menu when nobody was looking.) Eventually, both Rose and Enzo ended up in romantic dynamics with other people, but their intimacy remained intact. Rose remembers sitting on Enzo's sofa in her bra after a hookup, talking him through his feelings about somebody else, and asking, "How did we end up here?" She felt like he was an onion that she was peeling back, layer by layer, to reveal the sensitive soul underneath.

Rose and Enzo didn't see each other for years during the COVID-19 pandemic. When they reunited, he was married with a baby, and she was engaged. Since Enzo ended up with a woman he'd loved for a long time, with whom Rose had helped him forge a relationship despite significant obstacles, she felt like she had guided him to his happy ending, even though he had been the older, more confident one in their relationship while she was "a young girl figuring out life." When they first reunited, Rose held up her hand to show her engagement ring and said, "it's weird, right?" In response, Enzo flashed his wedding band and said, "it's very weird." While ultimately Enzo wasn't *her* Prince Charming, Rose has a sense of satisfaction—and, indeed, a feeling of reciprocal love—when she thinks about her experiences with this "cocky playboy."

While she remembers her Darcy experiences less fondly than Rose does, Winnie tells me that her involvement with the Darcy myth led her into the arms of her forever love. Winnie is a queer woman in her early thirties who had two extended relationships with

Darcy figures before she met her fiancé. Her first Darcy, Sean, was a boy she went to high school with. "He was arrogant and thought he was the coolest," Winnie explains, "and so did I." They were friends for a while, then had an unexpected hookup in a bucolic outdoor spot. Winnie explained how "it went back to an unrequited situation for years" until Sean, who was under the influence of hard drugs at the time, sent her a bunch of texts saying things like "you know me better than anyone else, we're the same person, we want the same things, and I wouldn't be me without you." Winnie says that she and Sean "had a lot of (terrible in retrospect) sex for a couple of months, but never really became an official couple. Then we both went to college and I realized he really was arrogant, self-centered, and not very cool, and that was the end of it."

In college, Winnie met her second Darcy, Chantal. Winnie told me that "Chantal was the coolest—made incredible art, was the life of the party, took care of their friends, knew about music and art and history. I was in big, unrequited love with them." Chantal had a long-term girlfriend, however, so Chantal and Winnie "flirted on the edge of friendship and something deeper." Then, one summer, Winnie went to Europe, and Chantal texted her incessantly while she was away. When Winnie got back to the US, she and Chantal had a steamy reunion that blossomed into something more. "Then we dated for years," Winnie explains, "moved in together, made life plans together, thought we were gonna get married, whole shebang. But turns out they were actually truly selfish, arrogant, and manipulative so we had a terrible, messy, months-long breakup and now don't speak."

At this point, Winnie's sister, Flora, chimes in: "Chantal also did the thing that dream Darcys do where they ultimately professed their undying love and offered everything that Winnie had been trying to commit to with them, Matthew Macfadyen and Kiera Knightley on the moors style . . . but only after Winnie was in a healthy, committed relationship," and Winnie confirms that this is true, calling it "wild and shitty and manipulative." "Turns out Darcys IRL are pretty shitty," she says.

Winnie tells me that these experiences with partners she had to chase and win and could never really count on were the two main love stories of her life before she met her "current and forever partner," Sally. Regarding her forever love, Winnie says, "Sally is the anti-Darcy in a lot of ways: not arrogant, doesn't come from this super academic life, very humble. But she's ended up being the real Darcy—gives me adventure, a dreamy future, totally requited, secure love. So, in total, Darcy is a fictional character and usually people are one half of him or the other, but rarely both and books are a bitch for making us think we can get everything in one person."

While Winnie's experiences with Darcy types didn't ultimately end in romance, they did lead her to her happily ever after and taught her what to look for in a prospective partner. Winnie adds that "it is truly wild how these character narratives get in your head and make you think it's gonna come true for you. Had it not been for all the magical endings I'd seen in books, movies, poetry, etc., I probably would have recognized far earlier that Sean and Chantal weren't my person. But for so long I held onto this ideal that they'd come around, the love would bloom, the dream would come true. But then even when the 'dream' did come true, it wasn't like the books or movies. It was manipulative and selfish. Thesis: the people who love you will show you from the start and if they don't it ain't real." I mean, I'm an English professor, so I love when someone tells me their thesis, and this one is so good. Agreeing with her sister, Flora chimes in to add, "My goal as a mom when it comes to teaching my daughter about relationships is that if you are in a situation where you are like, 'they just don't understand our love,' then it is not a relationship and you are not in love." The sisters talk about Big and Carrie in *Sex and the City*, about *Jane Eyre* and *Bridget Jones's Diary* and *Miss Congeniality* and *Grease*. And it is a beautiful thing to behold: two sisters and a little baby girl taking apart the Darcy myth like a line of knitting that has gone awry, winding the yarn back in order to create something new.

And maybe this is one step toward divesting from the Darcy myth: simply telling our stories to each other and retelling them to ourselves so that we can see how our actions and perceptions have been shaped by damaging cultural tropes. Once we have done that, maybe we can begin to write some new fairy tales together.

12

Darcy
and Other

ELIGIBLE

BACHELORS

or, Binge-Watching

the Myth

ride and Prejudice is just a book, but the Darcy myth has become foundational to the stories we tell about love and romance. By reaching back through the socially and politically engaged trend of Gothic writing, returning to a more realistic storytelling style, and then sharpening her wit and perfecting her vibe, Jane Austen wrote novels that go down like spun sugar but are also full of trap doors and secret monsters. By forgetting about her dark side—or by ignoring it—we have gotten horror mixed up with our romance for generations. And because art is powerful, and because we think of Jane Austen's stories as realist, or representative of real life, we have done this not only with the books we read and the movies we watch but in our real lives, too.

This might be true for you *even if* you have never read Jane Austen, because her works—especially *Pride and Prejudice*, and especially the Lizzy-Darcy dynamic—have had an outsize influence on British and American popular culture over the past couple of centuries. So, while some of us—my nerdy friends, especially—might get our ideas about love straight from a Jane Austen novel, we also get exposed to the Darcy myth via *When Harry Met Sally* or that Nancy Meyers movie where Jack Nicholson is dating Diane Keaton's daughter or *Dawson's Creek* or *Gossip Girl* or *Fifty Shades of Grey* or *Vampire Academy* or . . . you get the idea. Darcy is fucking everywhere, teaching us dangerous lessons: that it's our job to fix problematic partners; that we should expect to dislike and even distrust our love interests at first; and that falling in love is best savored when it follows a slow-burn, enemies-to-lovers arc. We're conditioned to try to "fix" people—often men—who we probably shouldn't be messing with in the first place. We're not just taught to love a beast, but told from a young age that turning a beast into a prince is exactly what love does, and what love is about.

Now, art and life mirror each other whether or not the art in question is particularly "realistic." (For example, *Beauty and the Beast* and *Twilight* sell us a particularly shiny version of the Darcy myth even though we recognize them as fantasy.) That said, Jane Austen became the OG influencer in part because she was so *relatable*—because her first generations of readers were convinced, both by her cozy style and by influential reviews and accounts of her life and work, that her characters were, or were just like, people they knew from real life. When fantasy hews too closely to reality, sussing out the lie can become a dangerous game.

As the interviews in the previous chapter demonstrate, the Darcy myth can get in our heads and mess with our expectations of ourselves and others in a variety of ways. We might take people at their word when they declare their love for us without pausing to wonder if they might be feeding off us vampirically, for example: trying to break up our current relationship not because they truly feel that they are meant to be with us but just to feel that they are in control. We might decide that it is our responsibility to fix someone, even if that person is unable or unwilling to change, and even if the trauma they've experienced is too great to be healed by our charms alone. We might even convince ourselves that the red flags we see in a potential partner are a failure of our perception and not our gut telling us to get the fuck out. While our own Darcy might be out there, the Darcy myth playbook isn't designed to help us find them. Rather, it's a monstrous, patriarchal tool, one that keeps us trapped and perennially disappointed, ready to move on to the next beast, whose power our love only feeds.

One way to put the Darcy myth in its place might be to separate fiction from reality. This is what I was getting at when I talked about reading *Pride and Prejudice* as a fairy tale. If we recognize that Darcy is Darcy but most people who show us red flags are *not* Darcy, then perhaps we can claim what we love about Darcy and seek that out in a potential partner without assuming that our relationships should follow the Darcy model. For example, you can try to find someone who is nice to their siblings without necessarily expecting to find that trait hidden deep within the sexy, complex psychology of someone who insults you the moment they see you, judges your family, convinces their friend to ghost someone you care about, etc. There's actually no correlation between being a good brother and being a douchebag. This is a made-up correlation that we've learned from a complicated character who Austen came up with while she was combining marriage plots with monster stories—but who, over the course of literary and cultural history, got elevated to the status of Ideal Man.

If we're thinking about how to resist the Darcy myth in our real lives, then a good first step might be separating out Darcy's swoon-worthy traits (when he says "my affections and wishes have not changed, but one word from you will silence me forever"— OMG!) from his more troubling ones. But this is hard to do in a cultural moment when the line between fiction and reality is becoming increasingly thin.

Now I am going to talk about *The Bachelor.*

I first started watching *The Bachelor* in the early days of my marriage, when my husband's dissertation research took us to New Orleans. He was embedded with a group of young activists (his degree is in anthropology), and they held a lot of their formal and informal group activities at night. I became friends with them too, and went out with the group frequently (Thursday nights on Frenchmen Street, I will never be that cool again), but I also found myself home alone a fair amount, in a city that was new to me. I got a little into cooking, and a lot into television. And the algorithms decided that I—like anyone who was watching TV—would probably love *The Bachelor.*

And love *The Bachelor* I did. Brad Womack (not, as the internet has informed me, to be confused with his twin brother, Chad Womack), was my first, even though it was not *his* first time being the Bachelor. Apparently, I learned, he had appeared on a previous season, but had decided not to choose either of the two finalists in the competition to be his wife. This season promised to have it all: A wife competition! A redemption arc! And a boss-level challenge to tame the savage bachelor beast!

Now, *The Bachelor* is Gothic and patriarchal to its core. Like, it's a wife contest *and* a story about a bunch of women trapped in a mansion. There's a moment that haunts me from one of the final episodes of Rachel Lindsay's season of *The Bachelorette*. She was sitting with the then host, Chris Harrison, whom she would later be instrumental in ousting from the franchise. It was one of those episodes where the host and the star watch scenes together and talk to castmates and each other. Rachel asked, "Can I leave?" and Chris assured her, "you can't leave."

I love *The Bachelor* and its various spin-off series (including the one where they had to sing, which was instrumental to my emotional health during the first summer of the COVID-19 pandemic). I don't consider this a guilty pleasure. First of all, I'm a Taurus; I don't feel guilty about my pleasures. Second, I recognize that both romance and the Gothic—two genres that commingle in the various Bachelor franchise shows—are easy to dismiss because they are easy to code as feminine. And Jane Austen taught me to take that shit seriously.

Naturally, feminists have wondered why some feminists like *The Bachelor*. In a 2017 article for *Vogue* titled "Why Feminists Are Unabashedly Obsessed with *The Bachelor*," Michelle Ruiz calls the show a "feminist nightmare" while suggesting that "beneath the avalanche of rose petals, many see a bizarre societal case study." Despite the appeal of claiming to perform a sociocritical hate-watch on the regular, Ruiz admits that "some of the *Bachelor/Bachelorette*'s feminist faithful concede that they aren't always watching through a critical lens, nor do they consider themselves entirely above the tearful trials of the show." Ruiz is certainly right that I'm not hate-watching; why would I watch something I hate? But I don't think enjoying the franchise is the same as completely disconnecting my analytical faculties. Rather, I would argue that my love for *The Bachelor* falls right in line with my critical work, because the pleasure of *The Bachelor*

How the Characters of *Pride and Prejudice* Would Fare in Bachelor Nation

CAROLINE BINGLEY would be accused of not being there "for the right reasons," and sent home after a dramatic two-on-one date. She would then capitalize on the exposure to become a successful fitness influencer.

LYDIA BENNET would get slut-shamed all over social media but would go on to star in *several* seasons of *Bachelor in Paradise*.

JANE BENNET would get a talking to about "opening up" and "being vulnerable."

MR. DARCY, much like Brad Womack, would probably need multiple seasons in order to make his selection.

MR. COLLINS would be genuinely confused to find himself having beef with other guys in the house, would be put on *Bachelor in Paradise* for a redemption arc, and would propose to Mary Bennet during the first week of the show.

MR. BINGLEY would be a terrible bachelor because he'd believe all the gossip and send nice women home just because other women decided to talk shit about them.

MRS. BENNET would be an extremely annoying yet effective producer.

and its family of shows is something like a Gothic pleasure. Think about it: The Bachelor mansion embodies the patriarchal structures we live under as a literal chandeliered, cavernous, very large house, a strange space haunted by the past—both by the various contestants' personal traumas (the revelation of past trauma as a tool for forging deeper intimacy is a major trope on the show) and by all the drama that has gone down in previous seasons. The contestants are met with various pressures—the producers, who function as unseen, almost supernatural forces from the viewer's perspective; good ol' competition; "villain" figures among the contestants; and sometimes physical challenges, like boxing, or cultural challenges, like performing stand-up comedy. There is, at every moment, the possibility that the norms of the show will be subverted, or that somebody will be better or more honest or more radical than their abs led us to expect—either that or way, way worse. There are strict rules but also, in a way, there are no rules, because this is the game of love. (And yes, I know about the show *Unreal*, which draws out the show's Gothic nature, situating the story of its production within a tale of absolute human depravity—but I will take candy-coated terror Gothic over horror Gothic any day of the week.)

In a 2014 essay aptly titled "The Marriage Plot," Roxane Gay writes that "in both darker and lighter versions of fairy tales, a woman's suffering is demanded in exchange for true love and happily ever after. She must be trapped in a tower or poisoned by an apple or forced to spin straw into gold. She must wait for the hand of a man who is fooled not once but twice before he finds her. Throughout any given season of *The Bachelor*, the women exclaim that the experience is like a fairy tale. They suffer the machinations of reality television, pursuing—along with several other women, often inebriated—the promise of happily ever after. Instead of bleeding from the foot to fit a golden slipper, they bleed their dignity, one episode at a time." Gay goes on to explain that, even though she knows "how damaging fairy tales are for women, how much sacrifice is demanded for an all-too-fragile promise of love," she still watches the show, suspending her disbelief and muting her feminism.

My consumption of *The Bachelor* is less self-aware. While I would love to say that, since that first season, I have curled up with popcorn and either live-tweeted every episode or shared it with a dedicated group of friends, that would make me sound way more organized and socially successful than I am. Rather, I don't watch every hour or every episode or even every season of the show—but I am always following it, the way some people follow sports.

But this is where I lose my grip on reality. Because the shows in the Bachelor franchise are "reality" shows—obviously they are heavily produced, and the people who go on them are signing up to be B-list celebrities, and the situations in which the producers place the cast are not realistic. But the people are real, and they are playing themselves, and these days they are on social media, continuing to play out their personas—however curated they may be—in the actual world. So I can follow a relationship trajectory, such as it is, from an episode I watched to a podcast recap to Instagram stories. Inevitably there's a breakup, and the breakup feels real, because these people are real and have feelings. Because of the unscripted nature of the show, and because of the way social media offers a glimpse into the ways in which relationships that formed on the show function afterward, *The Bachelor* is Gothic but it *feels* like realism. In other words, it functions much like a Jane Austen novel.

What is the effect of this blurring of reality and fiction on our psyches? What does it mean that, when I open a social media app, I see people I know living their lives, and then momfluencers I follow living perfectly curated, aestheticized versions of their lives, and then *Bachelor* cast members staying in character IRL? How is my brain supposed to understand the distinction between the marvelously messy realities of marriage and motherhood and the dominant, deeply patriarchal fictions of love and domesticity? How are we supposed to understand the difference between "reality" and reality?

We could take this analysis further, to the very definition of "authenticity" as a buzzword of the current era, or the way social media encounters can be designed to feel intimate or vulnerable. But the point I want to make is simpler than that. In a media climate where, recently, a persuasive TikTok video almost convinced me to paint self-tanner on my face in a clever contouring pattern, how can we expect to keep a tight hold on what's good advice and what's a vexed cultural trope? We need to get a handle on the Darcy myth now, before it's too late.

That's not easy to do, because the Darcy myth is sneaky as hell. Take the second season of the unfortunately named but very compelling social experiment/reality romance show, *Love Is Blind*. In it, the fabulously sharp and beautiful Deepti Vempati gets engaged, sight unseen, to Abhishek "Shake" Chatterjee, who turns out to be less of a prince than she'd hoped. In falling for him and accepting his proposal, Deepti falls for a Darcy myth hook, line, and sinker—and we can watch all of it.

In the very first episode of the season, we watch Shake ask a series of superficial questions to his potential love interests. The whole conceit of the show is that participants are talking to one another through a thin, opaque wall, so that they are discouraged from forming connections on the basis of looks and sexual attraction. But Shake asks questions designed to circumvent the restrictions of the show—asking, for example, if the person he's chatting with works out regularly, or if they're younger than he is.

When Shake connects with Deepti, they bond over the fact that they are Indian people who have dated predominantly blond partners. Shake tells Deepti that he is a veterinarian and house DJ, to which Deepti replies that she loves music. Shake asks, "if we were to be at a music festival, do you like being on a guy's shoulders?" Seeming to take this as face-value flirty banter, Deepti replies, "Yeah, you're up for the challenge, you can pick me up?" But then Shake makes his meaning very clear. He asks, "Yeah. But, um, will I have trouble picking you up?"

Lizzy Bennet that she is, Deepti calls him out on this, telling him that his comment "comes off very superficial." Later, to another cast member and to a producer, Deepti shares that this question was "very off-putting" and admits it's clear that "Shake places importance on the physical appearance."

In a later conversation, Deepti holds Shake accountable for his apparent superficiality. After he compliments her personality and calls her a "bubbly little woman," Deepti introduces the topic of his interest in her littleness. She asks, "did I ever tell you that I lost a ton of weight?" When Shake answers in the negative, Deepti clarifies, "like, close to, like, you know, seventy or eighty pounds probably."

In the Darcy myth where Deepti is living—or, at least, in the augmented version of "reality" in which Deepti is playing herself—this confession triggers a total Lizzy-Darcy moment. Shake displays shame and embarrassment over his shallowness. He explains that he was "chubby" growing up, and that he is used to dating somebody in shape in order to compensate for his bad body image. As a result of his experience on the show so far, he is learning that he "had more demons than he thought" in this department, and sees his superficial questions as a reflection of his own issues.

Ah yes, Deepti thinks, she is in a textbook romance plot, one in which she called a guy out on his shit and he apologized, took accountability for his past mistakes, and promised to be better. Except, he has *not* promised. Remember the wisdom fifteen-year-old Loden shared in the previous chapter: naming your faults is not the same as taking accountability for your actions.

But Deepti is deep in a Darcy myth, and so she tells Shake that his vulnerability makes her happy. They begin to discuss a future together.

Now, *Love Is Blind* perches on the knife's edge between fantasy romance and reality. I'm not sure we can really blame Deepti for thinking she's in a Darcy narrative. Boy meets girl. Boy insults girl. Girl calls boy on his shit while sharing some things about herself. Boy sees that his mistakes have been a result of past trauma. *Of course* it makes sense to Deepti that things are going to work out.

Pull the Darcy myth rug out from under this sketchy dude, however, and things get real. Boy meets girl. Boy asks girl if she needs to lose weight. Girl tells him she has lost a significant amount of weight, but seems annoyed at him. Boy says what he has to in order to save face, so that he doesn't lose this romantic prospect who has already told him that she is, if not small, then at least much smaller than she was, and willing and able to become smaller. To shrink to fit into his perception of himself, or his anxieties about how others perceive him. To extend him, expand him, stacking both her cultural and her literal, physical status on top of his shoulders, becoming a kind of monstrous expression of the things we give up when we overestimate our power to "fix" a problematic partner, and agree to chain ourselves to them for life.

Is it any surprise that Shake spends the rest of the season stressing out about how he isn't attracted to Deepti, and discussing this with the rest of the cast in deeply disrespectful ways? Is it any surprise that, during the show's denouement, when contestants decide whether or not to go through with their intended weddings, Deepti claims she is "choosing herself" when she leaves Shake at the altar? Even in the highly produced world of reality television, with cameras on the couple and microphones in their faces, we see that the Darcy myth falls flat when it comes to real people. The idea that Shake was going to overcome his superficiality because a smart girl told him about her weight loss hinges on the idea that somebody else is holding the pen—not the person himself but an author, a writer, someone who understands the generic contract implied in the romance genre, someone determined to get the audience their HEA.

The reality romance genre owes a debt to Austen, even if it can't always follow through on those kinds of promises, and some producers seem to know it. Some reality romance shows take their Darcy myths to the point of Anglophilia, as in the case of the short-lived and deeply problematic *I Wanna Marry "Harry,"* in which twelve American women were gaslit into thinking that the cute, regular guy whose affections they were competing for was, in fact, Prince Harry. And then there is *The Courtship.*

Now, as far as I can tell, the logic behind *The Courtship* is simply to combine two shows viewers already like—*The Bachelorette* and *Bridgerton*—into one show, in which a beautiful NFL cheerleader turned software engineer and her sixteen eligible suitors are "transported back to the most romantic era in history, that of nineteenth-century England." The logic, here, is the kind of logic that goes into the design of toddler cartoons, which often seems to start and end with the idea that two individual good things *must* be better together: Puppies in trucks! Dinosaurs on a train! Ocean life doing musical theater! And so forth.

Claiming that "in the search for true love looking for your future may lie in the past," the production makes very clear that the setting of *The Courtship* lies in "Jane Austen's times." To this end, the first episode of season one, sneakily titled "First Impressions" (there's a Janeite in the room for sure), opens with a bit of a thesis statement splashed across the screen: "It is a truth universally acknowledged that a single woman in search of a husband must go to Regency-era England and live in a castle with sixteen eligible suitors." This quote is attributed to "Jane Austen . . . *probably*." (Probably not!)

The Courtship indulges in a fantasy of Regency romance that glorifies the historical marriage market, imagining it as having been not about the consolidation of wealth and status but about love. Our "heroine," Ms. Nicole Rémy, tells us that "modern dating is not working" for her. She explains, "Courtship these days doesn't happen. It's really like, hooking up on a dating app and there's not the romance that you're looking for. And so, I'm ready to fall in love and find love like they did in Jane Austen novels. Back then, everything meant so much more, because it took time." When she meets her suitors, Ms. Rémy says, "We're in a Jane Austen movie. Like, we're in a fairy tale. And, along with that fairy tale is falling in love. And I hope that you guys can envision it with me too and we can ride away together on a carriage."

The tension between "the old ways of courtship" and the hypermodern world of a reality-TV dating competition is delicious. In the season premier, people quote Jane Austen; they also make jokes about corn dogs and TikTok.

Fast-forward to the season finale, when fans were disappointed to see the heroine choose Danny, whom some saw as uncommunicative and uncertain about their relationship, over the runner-up, Jesse, a fan favorite whom Nicole called "too safe." Unfortunately—but unsurprisingly, given the success rate of reality-TV romances—Danny proposed to Nicole in the season finale, took back the proposal a week later, and, a month later, broke up with her altogether. It turns out that not even a hyper-romanticized modern-meets-Regency version of reality in which she is quite literally the star of the show was enough to save our heroine from the Darcy myth.

But that doesn't mean it's too late, or that all is lost. Nicole Rémy is a beautiful twenty-seven-year-old with a thriving career and 15,800 Instagram followers, and if she wants a romantic partner, I'm sure she can take her pick. And as for the rest of us? We have this bone-deep reminder that reality is a bit of a porous concept, and that storylines from fiction influence how we see the world and how we respond to real-life situations. But we don't need to fall for the Darcy myth anymore. Much like the producers of reality television, we are free to drop the script.

13

Darcy on the
DOCKET

or, What Defining
Mr. Right Has to Do
with Our Rights

What does Mr. Darcy have to do with reproductive justice? More than you might think. Because our shared cultural conceptions about romance help keep us invested in a patriarchal social order that wants to take our rights away.

As we have seen, the figure of Mr. Darcy—the character, and more importantly the narrative surrounding him—provides cover for predatory, toxic behavior. Within the world of *Pride and Prejudice*, Darcy's decision to offer the financial incentive necessary to induce Wickham to marry Lydia Bennet lets Wickham off the hook for being a serial predator who has targeted young girls in his pursuit of money, power, and revenge. By essentially tying the knot *for* Wickham and Lydia, Darcy accomplishes his goal of making Lydia respectable again. This might be necessary for her own social health (although it might also be a lifelong punishment for a lapse in judgment she made at age sixteen), but Darcy tells Lizzy that, in making the marriage come together, he was thinking only of her. This can be read two ways. On one level, Darcy attempts to fix Lizzy's problem, both in order to ease her mind and because, by keeping the truth about Wickham's character quiet, he has partially caused the disaster of the kidnapping/elopement himself. But on another level, Darcy is keeping the Bennet family free from ruinous scandal so that, should Lizzy change her mind about his proposal (and surely this act of generosity will help move the needle), Darcy will be able to marry her without marrying into a family that has experienced social disgrace.

What Darcy has done for Lizzy with these actions might be loving and kind, and what he has done for or to Lydia is certainly complicated. But to fully understand the danger of the Darcy myth, we also need to look at what Darcy has done for Wickham. By paying off his debts and inducing him to marry Lydia, Darcy not only has saved Wickham from being known as a sexual predator but has in fact made him a respectable husband. Birth control being what it was in the nineteenth century, it's very possible that Wickham will also become a father soon; it's even possible that Lydia is pregnant already. So, by "saving" Lydia, Darcy has in fact reintegrated Wickham into the patriarchal social order. He has made him a husband and father, which makes him seem like a trustworthy avatar of the cultural powers that be. And he is an extension of those powers—it's just that those powers don't care one bit about, say, Lydia Bennet. (When Susan Collins voted to confirm Brett Kavanaugh to the US Supreme Court, despite the fact that he had been credibly accused of sexual assault, she called him a "husband and father," as if occupying those roles absolved him of his past sins rather than making him a legible player in a patriarchal status quo that doesn't give a fuck about teen girls like the ones he traumatized. And then she was all surprised when he voted to overturn *Roe v. Wade*.)

As an archetype and cultural icon, Darcy also provides cover for predatory behavior by training people—and, in particular, people that capitalist, white supremacist, heteronormative patriarchy would rather keep in their place—to think that a potential partner's mistreatment is in fact a little clue that will lead them to the consolation prize that is their great love story. The Darcy myth gives us a place to sink our energy that won't take anything away from the status quo and that will, in point of fact, allow people to mistreat us and to feed off our energy and efforts, at least for a little while. And the Darcy myth is an even dirtier trick than that, because it doesn't even do what it promises. Not only does the Darcy myth distract us from the real social change necessary to heal our communities by promising us an end run around the problem—forget destroying the patriarchy, just integrate yourself into the status quo by finding a hot husband!—but also the potential partners it points us toward are perfectly positioned, more often than not, to leave us high and dry.

The Darcy myth provides cover for Wickham's monstrosity in the world of Austen's novel, and it provides cover for general monstrosity in the real world. The Darcy trope informs our shared ideas of romance and of what kind of treatment we should accept from potential partners. If we zoom out, we see that the Darcy myth also helps to prop up and fortify a very Gothic, patriarchal universe that is, and always has been, scary for anyone who is not a very particular type of man. After all, if we are trained from childhood to invest ourselves in men who treat us poorly, aren't we more likely to end up in abusive situations and under threat of assault? If girls are taught that their purpose is to "fix" people who are "broken," then doesn't that lend credence to subcultures that claim that access to women's love and care should be a right?

But a world built to lock women in the attic will never be a world in which we are all free. And if a woman's job, in the Gothic real world in which we live, is to get interpolated into her predetermined roles as a wife and mother, or else left for (socially, if not physically) dead, then what are we to make of someone who claims control of their own body and their own future? Of a person who makes their own choices about when and whether to have children in a deeply unjust, calamitous world?

In Mary Wollstonecraft's unfinished novel, *The Wrongs of Woman, or Maria*, several characters realize that their personal conditions and positions within a bleak, patriarchal, Gothic universe cannot support the act of mothering. One commits suicide while pregnant and another swallows an abortifacient, while a third, the titular Maria, chooses to claim ownership and custody of her daughter. This radical reclamation of maternal authority leads her to be confined in a private asylum; as far as we can tell given the fragmentary nature of the manuscript, she never sees her daughter again.

Maybe Jane Austen included some coded abortions in her novels, and maybe she didn't. (I think she did.) Maybe her fallen women, in the margins of happily ever after, are intended as warnings, or maybe Austen thought they got what they deserved, or maybe we're supposed to read them as tragic figures. Maybe Jane Austen's beloved sister, Cassandra, gave birth to a child she'd conceived with her fiancé before he sailed away to make his fortune and died, or maybe she didn't. One thing that's certain is that if Cassandra had this little baby, she would have had to hide him, and so we will never know for sure.

Remember Winnie and Flora, the sisters who shared their Darcy experiences with me back in Chapter 11? Let's return to where we last left them, chatting about the Darcy myths that had informed their romantic educations. Winnie and Flora brought up Lauren and Jason's relationship in the old-school reality series *The Hills* and the song "Teenage Dirtbag." And then they decided that *Dirty Dancing*, which has been my favorite movie for as long as I can remember, is the anti–Darcy myth.

Now, far be it from me to claim that *Dirty Dancing* is some perfect, unproblematic work of cinema. I mean, it's as much about Jewish American class anxiety as it is about anything, and it's also relatively whitewashed. Patrick Swayze and Jennifer Grey allegedly didn't get along while filming, which accounts for a slightly Darcy-ish sexual tension between them, even if the plot hews more closely to other romance tropes (forbidden love across class and cultural differences, for example) than it does the one we've been focused on. Supporting her claim that the movie is an anti–Darcy myth, Flora explained, "What I love about *Dirty Dancing* is that there are some similar archetypes at play—he's older, more worldly, seems aloof and unavailable, she's younger, headstrong but naïve—but the power dynamics are also flipped by the class aspects of the story, and they quickly move beyond archetypes by learning about and loving and defending each other as whole people."

In *Dirty Dancing*, Baby—an ambitious young woman who wants to make a difference in the world—vacations with her family at a Borscht Belt resort. She ends up at a staff party where she encounters

Johnny, a working-class dancer and dance instructor at the resort, and her attraction to him is immediately palpable. Johnny's good friend and dance partner, Penny, is pregnant, and does not want to be. (The father is an asshole—an Ivy League medical student and womanizer working on the resort's wait staff for the summer.) Baby borrows money from her father to pay for Penny's abortion, and Johnny starts teaching Baby how to dance so that she can stand in for Penny in an important performance. When the abortion goes awry and Baby needs to call in her father for medical help, he assumes Johnny is responsible for Penny's pregnancy and tells Baby to stay away from him. But nobody puts Baby in a corner, and she shares her feelings with Johnny, beginning a romantic relationship with him. The pair continue to stand up for and beside each other despite further obstacles.

What's so beautiful about *Dirty Dancing*, to me, is that it's a movie about dancing and sex and ambition and class and family camp and forbidden romance, but all those things orbit around an act of community care, which is, very specifically, the shared project of procuring an abortion, and then the act of procuring additional medical care when that abortion proves to be unsafe—because safe abortion, in the world of the movie and increasingly in our world, is not legal.

The romantic love story in *Dirty Dancing* plays out between Baby and Johnny, but there are other love stories at play too. There is Johnny's deep platonic love of his dance partner Penny, one that insists on and protects her reproductive autonomy. There is Baby's access, by virtue of her class status, to capital and healthcare, and her willingness to leverage these privileges, when necessary, to help another woman maintain custody of her own body. There is the love story between Baby and her father, who needs to heal his protective instincts and classism and fear of what might happen when his children come into contact with the world, but who also gives what he has to give when it is needed, and who takes back misplaced gifts and unjust words when he realizes that he was wrong. Remember

Jen's therapist from Chapter 11, the one who said that if a love story doesn't look like a Darcy story, it's just a Darcy story you don't recognize? Maybe that applies, here, to Baby's relationship with her dad. Baby's father, Jack, is a patriarch with his own pride and prejudices, but he knows that Baby wants to change the world, starting with her little corner of it. For him, change takes time, but he ultimately consents to examining his preconceived notions. These acts of transformation, of connection, and, indeed, of love, issue from Penny's independent decision not to be pregnant.

And this is what makes *Dirty Dancing* so remarkable, and such a potent antidote to the Darcy myth—the interplay between independence and interdependence, and the recognition that many different types of love, not just sweep-you-off-your-feet romantic love, are worthy of care, attention, and reparative work. Baby pursues her equitable, respectful, honest relationship with Johnny without waiting for her father to approve of it. She comes to Johnny's rescue when he is accused of a petty crime, making clear that she was with him at the time of the alleged incident, even though this confession has ramifications for both of them. Baby gives her father her truth, and stands in the light of her own decisions. Jack eventually comes around out of a combination of unconditional love for his daughter, the ability to respect the wisdom of his wife, and an openness to new information that causes him to examine his prior assumptions. He is thus able to grow and change and become worthy of an honest relationship with Baby. But if Jack hadn't done this work—if he had failed—it would not have changed Baby's love story in the slightest. Because the Darcy myth teaches us to suck up to the patriarchy, while Baby—who combines youthful idealism with a propensity toward decisive action—has chosen to cast her lot with the future she and her community create together.

Being a person in a body that can create other bodies is an inherently Gothic state. Your body has the potential to be a cavernous, empty space, a place the future comes from. Whether this feels like a state of monstrous entrapment or radically generative creativity has a lot to do with your ability to make your own choices about how you populate the future, and with what that future looks like. At the end of *Dirty Dancing*, Jack tells Johnny, "When I'm wrong I say I'm wrong." Admitting to his faults and flaws, Darcy tells Lizzy that his mistakes were "unpardonable." In an era when those of us in the United States reel from the loss of our great freedom of bodily autonomy, an era after predators donned judicial robes and decreed that people—adults and children alike—should be forced to incubate and birth children whom the nation refuses to protect, it is urgent that we rethink our tropes and mythologies. This is particularly crucial when it comes to all types of love (including self-love) and the freedom to act on, express, and honor that love—and especially when it comes to the question of what we might owe each other. What it means to reconsider a deeply held belief, and admit that one was wrong. What it means to imagine romantic love not as an end in itself or a way out but as a meaningful and fortifying byproduct of just, inclusive networks of community care.

On a Friday afternoon in September 2022, University of Idaho employees received an email informing them that any discussion of abortion or birth control that was not completely neutral could result in dismissal, bars on future state employment, fines, or even jail time. Since the overturning of *Roe v. Wade*, abortion care is now banned in the state of Idaho with exceptions for cases of rape, incest, or life-threatening pregnancy; the university warned faculty that "academic freedom is not a defense to violation of law" and cautioned staff against "promoting" abortion in the course of doing their jobs.

   This demand isn't just evil, it is in fact impossible. Because, even when it's conveniently apolitical, as Austen's novels in particular might be, literature is never neutral. And readings of literature are never neutral—we don't go to literature to be neutral. That's not what literature is for.

Pride and Prejudice is a classic for a lot of reasons, and we can come to it for a lot of things. For a swoon-worthy romance plot. For sentences so intricate they wrap around us like a cozy scarf. For its coded engagement with the Gothic and with questions of women's precarity.

And perhaps, at this moment of crisis in the field of reproductive justice, we need to come to *Pride and Prejudice* in order to examine our very definitions of love and care, and the question of what our love and care are serving. Do we want our love to be in service of a very specific, Darcy-coded type of marriage plot, one in which we win because we find the best and most lucrative love available and use it to integrate ourselves into the social order? Or do we want our love and our care to be in the service of collective healing, collective freedom, collective joy? If we choose the latter—and I think we should—then we need to reimagine those tropes and archetypes that influence our thoughts and actions, sometimes without our conscious knowledge. And, just to be clear, we can still get married! But if we understand our romantic relationships as a microcosm of the world we hope to help create, then we'd better stop viewing potential partners through the Darcy filter, which is, basically, a trap. Because myths like the Darcy myth determine how we abdicate our power on the personal level, which is always, ultimately, political. And love should never be about abdicating our power, but rather about stepping into our power. About seeing one another as complex individuals with valid needs and unique desires. About building homes and lives and communities and families that truly represent who we are and what we hold dear.

Abortion in Eighteenth- and Nineteenth-Century British Literature

Jane Austen's crowd-pleasing marriage plots may include some coded references to abortion, but plenty of fiction from the period is much more explicit. There's a range of emotional and intellectual reactions to abortion in these novels; characters are sometimes horrified by the concept, sometimes relieved, sometimes a combination. But it's clear that abortion was part of people's lives in eighteenth- and nineteenth-century England just as it is today.

MOLL FLANDERS BY DANIEL DEFOE (1722)

In *The Fortunes and Misfortunes of the Famous Moll Flanders*, *Robinson Crusoe* author Daniel Defoe spins the tale of a woman born to a convict who, finding herself widowed, attempts to con men into thinking she is a widow of fortune so that she can marry well. At one point in the narrative, Moll is offered an abortifacient, which she rejects: "she could give me something to make me Miscarry, if I had a desire to put an end to my Troubles that way; but I soon let her see that I abhorr'd the Thoughts of it . . ."

ANTI-PAMELA BY ELIZA HAYWOOD (1741)

In *Anti-Pamela: or, Feign'd Innocence Detected*, Eliza Haywood offers a satirical response to Samuel Richardson's didactic novel *Pamela; or, Virtue Rewarded*. Richardson's Pamela is innocence personified, but Haywood's anti-Pamela, Syrena Tricksy, is only pretending. At a young age Syrena receives an abortion from her mother: "all that could be done, was to endeavour to alleviate the Misfortune as much as possible: To that end, she prepared a strong Potion, which the Girl very willing drank, and being so timely given, had the desired Effect, and caused an Abortion, to the great Joy of both Mother and Daughter."

THE WRONGS OF WOMAN, OR MARIA
BY MARY WOLLSTONECRAFT (1798)

In Mary Wollstonecraft's unfinished Gothic novel, one of the main characters, Jemima, becomes pregnant after her employer rapes her. Realizing that her abuser will be able to claim custody of her child, she takes an abortifacient: "I hurried back to my hole, and, rage giving place to despair, sought for the potion that was to procure abortion, and swallowed it, with a wish that it might destroy me, at the same time that it stopped the sensations of new-born life, which I felt with indescribable emotion."

FRANKENSTEIN; OR, THE MODERN PROMETHEUS
BY MARY SHELLEY (1818)

Victor Frankenstein promises to create a female creature so that his original creature (who refers to himself as an abortion at the end of the novel) will not be entirely alone. But when he sees his original creature grin at the work in progress, Frankenstein reports that he "thought with a sensation of madness on my promise of creating another like to him, and, trembling with passion, tore to pieces the thing on which I was engaged."

Conclusion:

DARCY IN OUR HEARTS

*T*he way we structure our loves can determine how we design our lives. And the way we structure our lives determines how we engage with one another. Yes, Jane Austen's *Pride and Prejudice* is just one little classic novel, but divesting from the hold its central archetype has on our shared cultural understanding of love is in fact a radical act of liberation. We need to get free from Mr. Darcy so that we can invest our time and energy into making our lives better, and fairer, and safer. We need to give up the dream of fixing a problematic partner (and maybe even the dream of convincing a problematic politician to have a change of heart), so that we can relish the astounding project of reciprocal love, care for each other, and work toward building a better world.

Of course, there are things we might want to hold on to from the Darcy-Lizzy love story we've been fed all these years. There's their witty banter, and intellectual connection. Lizzy is willing to call Darcy on his shit, even though he's rich and powerful, and so, even though their union can never be a marriage of equals (because nineteenth-century patriarchy determines that Lizzy and Darcy can never be of equal status in the context of marriage), the dynamic between them is, at least, one in which neither party is afraid to speak their mind, and one in which both Lizzy and Darcy trust that they will be heard by the other person. There's a shared willingness, in the relationship, to admit when one's actions or perceptions were or are wrong. There are the close sibling relationships Lizzy and Darcy share with Jane and Georgianna respectively, relationships that underscore each character's ability to prioritize care, devotion, and protection for the people they love. There is also the dignified way that Darcy promises to respect Lizzy's decision, whether she chooses to marry him or not. And there is the extent to which Darcy and Lizzy complement one another, each making the other more mature, more effective, more ethical—in a word, better.

These are inspiring qualities to look for in a relationship. If one or more of these details from the Lizzy-Darcy paradigm speaks to you, then I invite you to pick it up and keep it close to your heart. Take it with you as you move forward. But there are other aspects of this myth that it is time to leave behind: namely, the conviction that we should seek out a difficult partner in need of "fixing." Repeat after me: Building a life with another person, should that be what you choose to do, is challenging enough. You do not need to seek out the additional challenge of a person who is not ready to love you, or to enter into an equal partnership, or to treat you with respect. Love is not more delicious when it is difficult to earn. That is a lie that is sold to oppress you. Love—real love, and the demands it makes on us—is enough of a challenge without additional, fabricated drama.

In the song "White Horse" from her early album *Fearless*, Taylor Swift insists that the relationship in question is not a Darcy myth, or, at least, not a story in that vein. "I'm not a princess," she admits, and "this ain't a fairy tale," and "this ain't Hollywood." Moving on from the potential lover who "let [her] down" in the "small town," the song promises that "I'm gonna find someone someday / Who might actually treat me well." After all, Taylor sings, this is a "big world."

This seems simple enough, but the act of divesting from the Darcy myth has the potential to be both personally liberating and politically progressive. Because when we follow the dominant social expectation that we will submit to disrespectful behavior while giving our time, energy, bodies, hearts, and minds to the project of fixing other people and earning love, we in fact prop up social and political systems that can be very damaging indeed. When we divest from the Darcy myth—by recognizing it for what it is, realizing how the Darcy trope has influenced our thinking about relationships and situations, sharing our stories with each other, and retelling our own stories with their governing archetypes in mind—we are able to see how our willingness to take shit from romantic partners translates into a willingness to take shit from society writ large. When we surrender our inclination to fight for love that's hard to earn—an inclination that we have been trained to honor—we stand in our assurance that we deserve love, and that we possess the strength, intelligence, and ability to work in the service of secure love that honors us as whole people. We deserve love, and can create and co-create that love just by virtue of being who we are. And once we see ourselves as worthy of love, and see that everyone deserves love that doesn't have to be earned, or chased, or gained under duress, then we can begin to work toward the project of ensuring equal rights for everyone—because the personal is always political, and the way we see ourselves and each other in the context of interpersonal relationships has broad ramifications for the society we build together. Put quite simply, breaking up with the book boyfriend who has been messing with our heads can function as an act of self-care and community care, and can be a first step toward working for a more just world, both for ourselves and for others.

Along these lines, some adaptations of Austen's classic tilt the stakes of the story toward questions of community health. For example, Ibi Zoboi's 2018 YA retelling *Pride: A* Pride and Prejudice *Remix* re-imagines *Pride and Prejudice* as a story about gentrification. The novel begins with a twist on Austen's famous opening line:

> It's a truth universally acknowledged that when rich people move into the hood, where it's a little bit broken and a little bit forgotten, the first thing they want to do is clean it up. But it's not just the junky stuff they'll get rid of. People can be thrown away too, like last night's trash left out on sidewalks or pushed to the edge of wherever all broken things go. What those rich people don't always know is that broken and forgotten neighborhoods were first built out of love.

With this welcome, Zoboi recasts the question of love in the novel in terms of the interpersonal histories that build communities and the connections within and among families that continue to make those communities home. Sure, there ends up being romance in the novel's plot, but the question of love extends beyond the bounds of romantic love, encompassing questions of class, family, education, and community care. Nikki Payne's 2022 novel *Pride and Protest* continues reinventing the novel in this vein, casting Lizzy and Darcy as (respectively) an activist DJ and the CEO of Pemberley Development.

Something else these adaptations offer is a transposition of Austen's whitewashed novel into more contemporary, racially and culturally diverse settings. As scholars including Patricia Matthew, Mary Favret, and Yoon Sun Lee have explored, Jane Austen's novels "give comfort to whiteness." What that means, in a nutshell, is that they focus in on very small groups of very specific people while ignoring that Regency England was a much more diverse world than our imaginations when we read *Pride and Prejudice* would have us believe.

With this in mind, I've started teaching *Pride and Prejudice* alongside an anonymous 1808 novel called *The Woman of Colour: A Tale*. This is a novel that Austen might have read or been aware of but which subsequently went out of print for two hundred years. In *The Woman of Colour*, a biracial heiress from Jamaica—the daughter of a slaveholder and an enslaved woman—crosses the ocean and comes to Regency England. She is orphaned, and, per the terms of her father's will, she must marry her cousin, and he must take her father's name, in order for Olivia (via her new spouse) to receive her inheritance. Olivia arrives in England, where she encounters racist microaggressions and responds with clarity, intellectual generosity, and an unflappable sense of self-worth and identification with those who are not yet free. Olivia is more than willing to take on the role of heroine in her marriage plot, and, though she doesn't know her cousin well, she easily falls in love with and marries him. Things take a very Gothic turn, however, when her cousin's first wife—a tragic heroine white to the point of ghostly translucence—turns out to be alive, separated from her husband by her betrayer's acts of evil cunning, and not dead, as he had previously believed. In response to this dramatic turn of events and to the nullification of her marriage, Olivia claims the status of widow, along with control over her inheritance, and returns to her homeland, rejecting the advances of another kind and eligible suitor on her way. In other words, in a move that might help us unravel the Darcy myth into its component parts, Olivia recognizes the moment her love story has become a monster narrative, and gets out of there, claiming widowhood as a way to take control of her assets and assure her personal autonomy.

Much like Olivia, we need to learn how to cut and run from relationship dynamics and dominant expectations that do not serve us. Olivia's patriarch—already a morally corrupt figure—sends her straight to the heart of a Gothic novel. If she is going to earn her inheritance, she must do as he says, and marry who his will dictates. But once it becomes clear that the love story waiting there will be star-crossed, Olivia reclaims herself, claims her inheritance, and heads back to Jamaica where, she tells us, she will "zealously engage" herself in what she understands to be social justice pursuits. There's a lot to critique in *The Woman of Colour: A Tale*, especially if the author is white; leading scholar Lyndon J. Dominique, who edited the text for the twenty-first-century reissue, thinks it was likely written by a Regency-era author who herself identified as a woman of color, but we can never know for sure. But there is also a lot to love in this alternate ending to the marriage plot. For perhaps we could say that Olivia gets a happily ever after of her own—one that involves not control and protection in marriage, but self-control, self-worth, the control of one's own body and assets, and the opportunity to devote one's energy and talents where one feels they are most needed.

Let me tell you what happened with the kitten. (You know, the one I told you about at the beginning of this book, the one in a juniper bush?)

Now, as I mentioned, I don't know much about cats, and I ran to my teenage neighbor's side less from the confident sense that I could help and more because the idea of rescuing a helpless little animal followed a storyline that had been important to me since childhood.

But I am not particularly graceful, or fast, and despite my willingness to submerge myself in a juniper bush, I didn't seem able to catch the kitten myself.

So here is what I did. I ditched the script, the narrative I'd been trained to expect and pursue—that of noble rescuer and helpless animal. I asked instead: what is important here? The idea of personally catching the kitten didn't feel important. Rather, I realized, what I valued in this scenario was getting the little kitten out of the cold so that it could spend the night someplace warm and begin to recover from its ordeal.

I called on my community, and my neighbors—experienced cat owners who have previously fostered kittens—were quick to answer the call. They actually owned a cat carrier, because unlike me they know something about cats, and somehow, with patience and kindness, they managed to catch the little kitten. They took her home, gave her kitten food (because they know what cats eat!), and set her up with a cozy bed and heating pad. Juniper, as we all decided to call her, stayed in their warm, cozy house with lots of love, attention, toys, and treats until she was ready to find her forever home.

While the stories we consume might proffer instruction manuals for how to use our love, it is crucial that we remember that love is a deeply powerful tool. It is a tool that we can use to enact good in unexpected ways, to contribute to our own happiness, and to help and protect others. We need to make sure we don't lose sight of this resource—that we aren't throwing our love away on the project of turning the beast into the prince, or trying to "fix" partners who mistreat us, or attempting to subdue the monster. Rather, divesting from the Darcy myth is one way in which we can reclaim this power, and invest it where we choose—in acts of personal and community care, in meaningful, interpersonal connection, and in working to tilt our world toward greater kindness, freedom, and peace. For it is a truth universally acknowledged that a liberated person in possession of a good heart must be in want of a full and fruitful life.

Notes

CHAPTER 1

20   *Sally Rooney writes about nothing else:* Gloria Fisk, "What Are Feelings For?" Post45, June 15, 2020, https://post45.org/2020/06/what-are-feelings-for.

20   *a man who treats you poorly is just hurt:* See Janice Radway, *Reading the Romance: Women, Patriarchy, and Popular Culture* (Chapel Hill: University of North Carolina Press, 1984, reissued 2009).

26   *and travel to Paris as husband and wife:* For more on Mary Shelley's involvement with Walter Sholto Douglas and Isabella Robinson, see Betty T. Bennett, *Mary Diana Dods, a Gentleman and a Scholar* (Baltimore: Johns Hopkins University Press, 1994).

CHAPTER 2

32   *"rather too light, and bright, and sparkling":* In a letter to her sister Cassandra dated "Thursday 4 February 1813," Austen writes, "—The work is rather too light & bright & sparkling;—it wants shade:—it wants to be stretched out here & there with a long Chapter—of sense if it could be had, if not of solemn specious nonsense—about something unconnected with the story; an Essay on Writing, a critique on Walter Scott, or the history of Buonaparté [*sic*]—or anything that would form a contrast & bring the reader with increased delight to the playfulness & Epigrammatism of the general stile.—I doubt your quite agreeing with me here—I know your starched Notions." Jane Austen, *Jane Austen's Letters,* edited by Deirdre Le Faye (Oxford, UK: Oxford University Press, 2011), 212.

CHAPTER 3

50   *make the reader feel* seen: Deidre Shauna Lynch, "Cult of Jane Austen," in *Jane Austen in Context*, edited by Janet Todd (New York: Cambridge University Press, 2005), 112.

50   *"she* likes *women":* Kathleen Anderson, *Jane Austen's Women: An Introduction* (Albany: State University of New York Press, 2018), xix.

53   *up to 38 percent of all published novels:* For more on the Gothic explosion, see Robert Miles, "The 1790s: The Effulgence of Gothic," in *The Cambridge Companion to Gothic Fiction*, edited by Jerrold E. Hogle (New York: Cambridge University Press, 2002), 41–62.

54   *as opposed to the terror Gothic:* For more on the distinction between terror and horror, see Ann Radcliffe, "On the Supernatural in Poetry. By the Late Mrs. Radcliffe." *New Monthly Magazine* (1826): 145–52.

55   *and puppies were brought in instead:* For more on Mary Shelley's birth and Wollstonecraft's death, see Cynthia Richards, "The Body of Her Work, the Work of Her Body: Accounting for the Life and Death of Mary Wollstonecraft," *Eighteenth-Century Fiction* 21, no. 4 (2009): 565–92.

58   *"characters that the reader cannot fail to recognize":* See "Review of Emma by Sir Walter Scott, *The Quarterly Review* (1815–1816)," in Jane Austen, *Emma*, edited by Kristin Flieger Samuelian (Peterborough, ON: Broadview Editions, 2004).

58   *"Aunt Jane":* Devoney Looser, *The Making of Jane Austen* (Baltimore: Johns Hopkins University Press, 2017), 4–5.

CHAPTER 4

66   *It's conceivable Austen is implying:* For more on this interpretation, see Peter A. Appel, "A Funhouse Mirror of Law: The Entailment in Jane Austen's *Pride and Prejudice*," *Georgia Journal of International and Comparative Law* 41, no. 3 (2013): 609–36.

CHAPTER 5

79   *or induce an abortion:* For more on the possibility of Marianne's coded pregnancy, see "Miscarrying the Marriage Plot," an essay I coauthored with eight brilliant University of Denver undergraduates (now alumnae): Julia Curry, Rose Frasier, Jenna Janssen, Andrea Jones, Anna Marie Oakley, Kathleen G. O'Donnell, Juliette Pisano, and Katherine White. The piece was first published in *Romantic Circles Pedagogies* (June 2021), and then reprinted in *Sensibilities*, the journal of the Jane Austen Society of Australia (June 2022).

80   "*fashionable novel*": Jan Fergus quotes Milbanke in "The Professional Wom-
      an Writer," in *The Cambridge Companion to Jane Austen,* edited by Edward
      Copeland and Juliet McMaster (Cambridge: Cambridge University Press,
      1997), 22.

CHAPTER 6

96   *stabbed the Beast in the back:* See Elizabeth Hopkinson, "Fairy Tales in Clas-
      sics—Pride and Prejudice vs. Beauty and the Beast," Silver Petticoat Re-
      view, September 26, 2002, https://www.silverpetticoatreview.com/fairy-
      tales-in-classics-pride-and-prejudice-beauty-and-the-beast.

CHAPTER 8

122   *he changes when he doesn't have to:* The idea that Darcy's change is more mean-
      ingful because he doesn't have to do it was first suggested to me in class by
      a student named Eleanor Carter.

125   "*the yearning that structured*": Claire Jarvis, *Exquisite Masochism: Marriage, Sex,
      and the Novel Form* (Baltimore: Johns Hopkins University Press, 2016), 27.

130   *pregnant brides were not uncommon:* For more on the history of pregnancy in
      England, see Richard Adair, *Courtship, Illegitimacy, and Marriage in Ear-
      ly Modern England* (Manchester: Manchester University Press, 1996) and
      Valerie Fildes, ed., *Women as Mothers in Pre-Industrial England* (New York:
      Routledge, 2013).

CHAPTER 9

139   "*angel in the house*": "The Angel in the House" is a poem by Coventry Pat-
      more.

140   *a medium in two senses of the word:* For more on haunted technology, Mina's
      channeling, and Victorian fiction, see Jill Galvan, *The Sympathetic Medi-
      um: Feminine Channeling, the Occult, and Communication Technologies, 1859–1919*
      (Ithaca: Cornell University Press, 2010).

141   *makes everything feel like a void for Bella:* Sarah Blackwood, "Our Bel-
      la, Ourselves," *Hairpin,* November 16, 2011, https://www.thehairpin.
      com/2011/11/our-bella-ourselves.

CHAPTER 10

154 *"love is the gift that keeps on taking":* See Lauren Berlant, *Cruel Optimism* (Durham: Duke University Press, 2011).

155 *really a history of translation:* Elizabeth Wanning Harries, *Twice upon a Time: Women Writers and the History of the Fairy Tale* (Princeton: Princeton University Press, 2001), 80.

156 *Pamela loses a shoe heel:* Alicia Kerfoot, "Virtuous Footwear: Pamela's Shoe Heel and Cinderilla's 'Little Glass Slipper,'" *Eighteenth-Century Fiction* 31, no. 2 (2019): 343–71.

156 *even more dangerous than their vicious animal counterparts:* Jack Zipes, *The Trials and Tribulations of Little Red Riding Hood* (New York: Routledge, 1993), 95–96.

CHAPTER 12

189 *"above the tearful trials of the show":* Michelle Ruiz, "Why Feminists Are Unabashedly Obsessed with *The Bachelor*," *Vogue*, January 10, 2017, https://www.vogue.com/article/why-feminists-love-the-bachelorette.

192 *suspending her disbelief:* Roxane Gay, "The Marriage Plot," *New York Times*, May 10, 2014, https://www.nytimes.com/2014/05/11/opinion/Sunday/the-marriage-plot.html.

CHAPTER 14

215 *Regency England was a much more diverse:* For more on this topic, see Patricia A. Matthew, "Jane Austen and the Abolitionist Turn," *Texas Studies in Literature and Language* 61, no. 4 (2019): 345–61; Mary A. Favret, "Frederick Douglass and *Pride and Prejudice*," *The Wordsworth Circle* 51, no. 3 (2020): 396–415; and Yoon Sun Lee, "Jane Austen, Whiteness, and the Phenomenology of Comfort," *Keats-Shelley Journal* 70 (2021): 111–17. To the best of my knowledge, the exact phrase "give comfort to whiteness" comes from a series of talks given by Mary Favret in 2017.

216 *we can never know for sure:* See Lyndon J. Dominique's "Introduction" to *The Woman of Colour: A Tale* (Peterborough, ON: Broadview Editions, 2008): 11–42.

Bibliography

Adair, Richard. *Courtship, Illegitimacy, and Marriage in Early Modern England*. Manchester: Manchester University Press, 1996.

Anderson, Kathleen. *Jane Austen's Women: An Introduction*. Albany: State University of New York Press, 2018.

Anonymous. *The History of Little Goody Two-Shoes*. In Lewis Carroll, *Alice's Adventures in Wonderland*, edited by Richard Kelly. Peterborough, ON: Broadview Editions, 2011.

————. *The Woman of Colour: A Tale*. Edited by Lyndon J. Dominique. Peterborough, ON: Broadview Editions, 2008.

Appel, Peter A. "A Funhouse Mirror of Law: The Entailment in Jane Austen's *Pride and Prejudice*." *Georgia Journal of International and Comparative Law* 41, no. 3 (2013): 609–36.

Ardolino, Emile, director. *Dirty Dancing*. Vestron Pictures, 1987.

Austen, Jane. *Emma*. Edited by Kristin Flieger Samuelian. Peterborough, ON: Broadview Editions, 2004.

————. *Emma*. Edited by Stephanie Insley Hershinow. New York: W. W. Norton & Company, 2022.

————. *Jane Austen's Letters*. Edited by Deirdre Le Faye. Oxford, UK: Oxford University Press, 2011.

————. *Jane Austen's Manuscript Works*. Edited by Linda Bree, Peter Sabor, and Janet Todd. Peterborough, ON: Broadview Editions, 2013.

————. *Mansfield Park*. Edited by June Sturrock. Peterborough, ON: Broadview Editions, 2001.

————. *Northanger Abbey*. Edited by Claire Grogan. Peterborough, ON: Broadview Editions, 2002.

————. *Pride and Prejudice*. Edited by Jenny Davidson. New York: W. W. Norton & Company, 2022.

————. *Pride and Prejudice*. Edited by Robert P. Irvine. Peterborough, ON: Broadview Editions, 2002.

————. *Sense and Sensibility*. Edited by Kathleen James-Cavan. Peterborough,

ON: Broadview Editions, 2001.

Bennett, Betty T. *Mary Diana Dods, a Gentleman and a Scholar*. Baltimore: Johns Hopkins University Press, 1994.

Berlant, Lauren. *Cruel Optimism*. Durham: Duke University Press, 2011.

Blackwood, Sarah. "Our Bella, Ourselves." *Hairpin*. November 16, 2011. https://www.thehairpin.com/2011/11/our-bella-ourselves.

Brontë, Emily. *Wuthering Heights*. Edited by Beth Newman. Peterborough, ON: Broadview Editions, 2007.

Burney, Frances. *Evelina: or, A Young Lady's Entrance into the World*. Edited by Susan Kubica Howard. Peterborough, ON: Broadview Editions, 2000.

Byron, George Gordon. *The Major Works*. Edited by Jerome J. McGann. Oxford, UK: Oxford University Press, 2008.

Curry, Julia, Rachel Feder, Rose Frasier, Jenna Janssen, Andrea Jones, Anna Marie Oakley, Kathleen G. O'Donnell, Juliette Pisano, and Katherine White. "Miscarrying the Marriage Plot." In *Teach (the) Romantic/Romantic Teaching, vol. 1*. Edited by D. B. Ruderman and Kate Singer. *Romantic Circles Pedagogies*. June 2021.

Coleridge, Samuel Taylor. "Christabel." *Poetry Foundation*. https://www.poetry-foundation.org/poems/43971/christabel

Defoe, Daniel. *Moll Flanders*. Edited by Paul A. Scanlon. Peterborough, ON: Broadview Editions, 2005.

Favret, Mary A. "Frederick Douglass and *Pride and Prejudice*." *Wordsworth Circle* 51, no. 3 (2020): 396–415

Fergus, Jan. "The Professional Woman Writer." In *The Cambridge Companion to Jane Austen*, edited by Edward Copeland and Juliet McMaster, 12–31. Cambridge: Cambridge University Press, 1997.

Fielding, Henry. *See* Haywood, Eliza, and Henry Fielding.

Fildes, Valerie, editor. *Women as Mothers in Pre-Industrial England*. New York: Routledge, 2013.

Fisk, Gloria. "What Are Feelings For?" *Post45*, June 15, 2020. https://post45.org/2020/06/what-are-feelings-for.

Galvan, Jill. *The Sympathetic Medium: Feminine Channeling, the Occult, and Communication Technologies, 1859–1919*. Ithaca: Cornell University Press, 2010.

Gay, Roxane. "The Marriage Plot." *New York Times.* May 10, 2014. https://www. nytimes.com/2014/05/11/opinion/Sunday/the-marriage-plot.html.

Harries, Elizabeth Wanning. *Twice upon a Time: Women Writers and the History of the Fairy Tale.* Princeton: Princeton University Press, 2001.

Harris, Charlaine. *Dead Until Dark.* New York: Ace Books, 2001.

Haywood, Eliza. *Fantomina and Other Works.* Edited by Alexander Pettit, Margaret Case Croskery, and Anna C. Patchias. Peterborough, ON: Broadview Editions, 2004.

———. *The History of Miss Betsy Thoughtless.* Edited by Christine Blouch. Peterborough, ON: Broadview Editions, 1998.

Haywood, Eliza, and Henry Fielding. *Anti-Pamela and Shamela.* Edited by Catherine Ingrassia. Peterborough, ON: Broadview Editions, 2004.

Hopkinson, Elizabeth. "Fairy Tales in Classics—Pride and Prejudice vs. Beauty and the Beast." Silver Petticoat Review, September 26, 2002. https://www. silverpetticoatreview.com/fairy-tales-in-classics-pride-and-prejudice-beauty-and-the-beast.

Jarvis, Claire. *Exquisite Masochism: Marriage, Sex, and the Novel Form.* Baltimore: Johns Hopkins University Press, 2016.

Keats, John. *The Major Works.* Edited by Elizabeth Cook. Oxford, UK: Oxford University Press, 2008.

Kerfoot, Alicia. "Virtuous Footwear: Pamela's Shoe Heel and Cinderilla's 'Little Glass Slipper.'" *Eighteenth-Century Fiction* 31, no. 2 (2019): 343–71.

Lee, Yoon Sun. "Jane Austen, Whiteness, and the Phenomenology of Comfort." *Keats-Shelley Journal* 70 (2021): 111–17.

Le Fanu, J. Sheridan. *In a Glass Darkly.* Edited by Elizabeth Tilley. Peterborough, ON: Broadview Editions, 2018.

Looser, Devoney. *The Making of Jane Austen.* Baltimore: Johns Hopkins University Press, 2017.

Lynch, Deidre Shauna. "Cult of Jane Austen." In *Jane Austen in Context,* 111–20. Edited by Janet Todd. New York: Cambridge University Press, 2005.

Matthew, Patricia A. "Jane Austen and the Abolitionist Turn." *Texas Studies in Literature and Language* 61, no. 4 (2019): 345–61.

Meyer, Stephenie. *Midnight Sun.* New York: Little, Brown and Company, 2020.

———. *Twilight.* New York: Little, Brown and Company, 2005.

Miles, Robert. "The 1790s: The Effulgence of Gothic." In *The Cambridge Companion to Gothic Fiction*, 41–62. Edited by Jerrold E. Hogle. New York: Cambridge University Press, 2002.

Piznarski, Mark, director, and Josh Schwartz and Stephanie Savage, writers. "Pilot." *Gossip Girl* season 1, episode 1 (2007). The CW.

Polidori, John William. *The Vampyre and Ernestus Berchtold; or, The Modern Oedipus.* Edited by D. L. Macdonald and Kathleen Scherf. Peterborough, ON: Broadview Editions, 2008.

Radcliffe, Ann. "On the Supernatural in Poetry. By the Late Mrs. Radcliffe." *New Monthly Magazine*, 1826, 145–52. Accessed via ProQuest.

Radway, Janice. *Reading the Romance: Women, Patriarchy, and Popular Culture.* Chapel Hill: University of North Carolina Press, 1984 (reissued 2009).

Richards, Cynthia. "The Body of Her Work, the Work of Her Body: Accounting for the Life and Death of Mary Wollstonecraft." *Eighteenth-Century Fiction* 21, no. 4 (2009): 565–92.

Richardson, Samuel. *Clarissa, or the History of a Young Lady.* Edited by Angus Ross. New York: Penguin Classics, 1985.

Rodrigo, Olivia. *Sour.* Geffen Records, 2021.

Ruiz, Michelle. "Why Feminists Are Unabashedly Obsessed with *The Bachelor*." *Vogue*, January 10, 2017. https://www.vogue.com/article/why-feminists-love-the-bachelorette.

Shelley, Mary. *Frankenstein.* Edited by D. L. MacDonald and Kathleen Scherf. Peterborough, ON: Broadview Editions, 2012.

Stoker, Bram. *Dracula.* Edited by Rachel Feder. New York: W. W. Norton & Company, 2023.

Swift, Taylor. *All Too Well: The Short Film.* Taylor Swift Productions and Saul Projects, 2021.

———. *Fearless (Taylor's Version).* Republic Records, 2021.

———. *Red (Taylor's Version).* Republic Records, 2021.

Taylor-Johnson, Sam, director. *Fifty Shades of Grey.* Universal Pictures, 2015.

Trousdale, Gary, and Kirk Wise, directors. *Beauty and the Beast.* Walt Disney Pictures, 1991.

Tsuchida, Steven, director, and Dan Harmon, writer. "Origins of Vampire Mythology." *Community* season 3, episode 15 (2012). NBC.

Wollstonecraft, Mary. *Mary, a Fiction and The Wrongs of Woman, or Maria.* Edited by Michelle Faubert. Peterborough, ON: Broadview Editions, 2012.

Zipes, Jack. *The Trials and Tribulations of Little Red Riding Hood.* New York: Routledge, 1993.

Index

Acknowledgments

This little book has been living rent-free in my head for years, and it's a thrill to thank the community that helped make it a reality. I honestly can't believe I was lucky enough to work with one of my all-time favorite writers and editors, Jess Zimmerman, who made this book approximately one million percent better, both in what she added and in what she cleared away. If you cut yourself on the argument, it's her fault for making it so much sharper. And Jess's comprehensive, exacting edits made me sharper, too.

It has been such a pleasure to work with the incredible team at Quirk. Jane Morley and Kassie Andreadis polished the text until it shone, Elissa Flanigan created the design of my wildest dreams, and I am so grateful to John McGurk, Mandy Sampson, Jennifer Murphy, and Nicole Valentino for ushering the book into the world and helping it find its people. My fabulous agent, Becky LeJeune, saw the heart and soul of this project from the beginning. She never tells me my ideas are too strange, and is there to support me no matter what comes up.

I'm grateful to the colleagues who lent their words and wisdom to this book, among them Gloria Fisk, Kathleen Lubey, Manushag Powell, Stephanie Insley Hershinow, and Nan Z. Da, and to those who offered support and insight behind the scenes, including Anne McCarthy, Lauren Burke, Eugenia Zuroski, Selah Saterstrom, Devoney Looser, and Doug Murray. Marjorie Levinson continues to remind me that thinking about literature should generate light and heat. Sarah Mesle and Sarah Blackwood offered a home, in *Avidly*, for an early essay toward this project, and Jamie Farquhar-Mueller generously shared her inspirational experiences teaching *Pride and Prejudice* in the high school classroom. To the anonymous interviewees who shared their Darcy experiences with me: I am so appreciative of your courageous acts of self-reflection. I would never have written this book, or tried my hand at nonfiction for a general audience, if not for the friendship and mentorship of McCormick Templeman, who sees the potential in everything and everyone and who illuminated the path every step of the way.

This book has an excellent cheering section, including but not limited to Sierra Shaffer, Sarah Ehlers, Sheera Talpaz, Rebecca Ariel Porte, Chet Lisiecki, Julie Steiner, Erin Hittesdorf, Sara and Ezra Rich, Julia Michie Bruckner, and my marvelous family by marriage, including my sisters-in-law Nomi, Yael, and Liba, along with their beautiful families, and my in-laws, George and Debby Kornfeld, the latter of whom will, I hope, share this with her writing group.

The Darcy Myth has grown out of many riveting conversations with many ingenious students over the course of many years. I am grateful for you all, and want to extend a special thank-you to the participants in my Autumn 2022 senior seminar, who so graciously added their insight and enthusiasm to this project, and who appear in its pages: Halli Ackley, Julia Best, Eleanor Carter, C.J. D'Amico, Kaylee Folger, Zoe Griscz, Nicky Gsell, Lyza Hecb, Irving Humphrey, Adreanna Jasso, Alexandra Kaufman, Adelaide Kennedy, Gretchen Knowles, Cameron Pecoraro, Sydney Pine, Bella Riedell, Cole Schwendeman, and Marlon Villeda-Galeano.

This book is dedicated to my mom and dad, Rob and Andee Feder, who are wonderful enough to deserve every dedication, but for whom a book about the power of rejecting dominant narratives, forging honest intimacy that defies expectation, and knowing your own mind is particularly fitting. They never let the world confuse me and they taught me to know my own worth and to say absolutely not, and for this I am eternally grateful.

My brother, Jed Feder, always lifts me up [insert muscle emoji], and teaches me to be louder and bolder and braver about my creative projects, and just in general. I'm thankful for his support of this and, indeed, all my endeavors. His wife, my brilliant sister-in-law Tiffany Tatreau, was instrumental to the book's development—I'm grateful to her for reading and rereading chapters and outlines and proposal materials, and for teaching me about Taylor Swift and Tik-Tok. If at any point in this book I come across as hip and with it, you've been duped, and it was all her doing.

The closer I get to my heart, the harder it is to find words, so I will just say that my husband, Moshe Kornfeld, cultivates a world in which I can be my most honest and therefore weirdest self. He created space and time for every single one of these pages to come into being. I am grateful to him—and to our sons, Nathaniel and Noah—together, the loves of my life.